Clifton Johnson

The New England Country

Clifton Johnson

The New England Country

ISBN/EAN: 9783337236373

Printed in Europe, USA, Canada, Australia, Japan

Cover: Foto ©ninafisch / pixelio.de

More available books at **www.hansebooks.com**

CONTENTS

PART I
OLD TIMES ON A NEW ENGLAND FARM ... 1

PART II
THE NEW ENGLAND OF TO-DAY ... 34

PART III
NEW ENGLAND AS THE TRAVELLER SEES IT ... 57

PART IV
CAMPING AMONG THE NEW ENGLAND HILLS ... 82

LIST OF ILLUSTRATIONS

	PAGE
JANUARY	*Frontispiece*
OLD FIREPLACE	1
A FOOT-STOVE	1
CANES AND UMBRELLAS	1
THE CHURN	2
YE ENTRANCE OF OLD FASHION	2
FARM TOOLS	2
A LOOM	3
FANS AND BACK-COMB	3
OLD CHAIRS	3
ONE OF THE OLD HOUSES	4
A SILHOUETTE PORTRAIT	5
A RIVER-BOAT BEFORE THE DAYS OF RAILROADS	5
REELS	6
A COMFORTABLE FARM-HOUSE	6
THE FLAX-WHEEL	6
FEBRUARY	7
KITCHEN UTENSILS	9
GOURDS AND PIGGINS	9
THE WINDING ROADWAY	10
A MILL-YARD IN THE VALLEY	11
A SUNNY GLEN	11
A QUIET DAY	12
A BARN-DOOR GROUP	13
A TURN IN THE ROAD	14
A NEW ENGLAND VALLEY	14
A HILLTOP VILLAGE	15
A LITTLE LAKE	16
A VILLAGE SCENE	17

LIST OF ILLUSTRATIONS

	PAGE
Snow-fields on the Hills	18
March	19
Cleared Land	21
Gathering Sap in the Sugar Orchard	22
Wayside Berry-pickers	23
A Farm amid the Big Hills	24
A Little Home on the Hillside	25
A Stream from the Hills	25
A Saw-mill	26
A Spring Morning	27
A Willow-lined River	28
April — One of the Old Village Streets	29
A Look down on the Connecticut	31
The Spring Hoeing	32
An Old Tavern	33
The Friendly Guide	34
A Hill Town	34
The Back Sheds	35
Winter Twilight — Going up for one more Slide	36
A Hill-town Village	37
Homes and Out-buildings by the Wayside	38
New England Rocks	39
Holding the Horses while his Father goes in to get a Drink of Water	40
May	41
A Dam on the Connecticut	43
At the Railroad Station	43
On the Outskirts of a Growing Factory Village	44
The Railway-crossing in the Village	45
A Stone Bridge	46
A Group of Little Fishermen	47
A Wayside Watering-trough	48
A Country School watching a Team go by	48
An Old Burying-ground	49
Below the Dam	50
A Massachusetts Mountain	51
The Ferryboat	51

LIST OF ILLUSTRATIONS

	PAGE
A Fall on the Connecticut	52
June	53
The Growing Boy in his Last Year's Clothes	. 55
At the Back-door .	. 55
The Academy . .	56
A Horse-chestnut Man .	57
Afterglow .	. 57
The Village Church . .	58
One of the Humbler Houses	59
A Deserted Home	59
Getting a Load of Sawdust back of the Saw-mill .	. 60
A Meadow Stream . .	60
A Home under the Elms	61
A Door-step Group	. 62
A Roadside Friend . . .	. 63
Better than Hoeing on a Hot Day	. 64
July	65
The Pet of the Farm .	. 67
The Big Barn-door .	. 68
The Boy who Mows away . . .	69
Summer Sunlight in a "Gorge Road" .	. 70
One of the Little Rivers	71
The Village Groceryman	72
An Outlying Village	73
A Village View in a Half-wooded Dell	74
The Old Well-sweep	. 75
In Haying Time	76
The Stream and the Elms in the Meadow	77
Under the Old Sycamore	78
August . . .	79
The Brook in the Woods	81
The House with the Barn across the Road	82
A Warm Summer Day	83
At Work in her Own Strawberry Patch .	84
September	. 85
Evening	. 87
A Load of Wood on the Way up to the Village	88

LIST OF ILLUSTRATIONS

	PAGE
A Waterfall in the Woods	89
A Panorama of Hills and Valleys	90
A Pasture Group	91
October	93
A Pasture Gate	95
A Road by the Stream	96
At the Pasture Gate	97
The Sheep Pasture	98
A Quiet Pond	99
Husking-time	100
Sunlight and Shadow	101
November	103
The Village on the Hill	105
A Mill in the Valley	106
Cloud Shadows	107
A Log House	109
A Farm-yard Group	110
On a Mountain Crag	111
One of the Green Mountain Peaks	111
Among the Big Hills	112
A Deserted Hut in the Woods	113
Charcoal Kilns	114
Rough Uplands	115
December	117
A Path in the Winter Woods	119
Windy Winter — On the Way Home from School	120

x

OLD FIREPLACE

PART I

OLD TIMES ON A NEW ENGLAND FARM

A FOOT-STOVE

ABOUT "old times" there always hovers a peculiar charm. A dreamland atmosphere overhangs them. The present, as we battle along through it, seems full of hard, dry facts; but, looking back, experience takes on a rosy hue. The sharp edges are gone. Even the trials and difficulties which assailed us have for the most part lost their power to pain or try us, and take on a story-book interest in this mellow land of memories.

To speak of "the good old times" is to gently implicate the present, and the mild disapproval of the new therein suggested is, from elderly people, to be expected. We grow conservative with age. Quiet is

CANES AND UMBRELLAS

more pleasing than change. The softened outlines of the past have an attraction which the present matter-of-fact hurry and work have not, and the times when we were young hold peculiar pleasure for our contemplation. To actually prove by logic and rule that the old times were better than the new would not be easy. They had their lacks. The world learns and gains many things as it ages. It is to be hoped that it grows better as it grows older; but even so the past has its charm, whether one of memories in which we ourselves were actors, or of story, which shows the

THE CHURN

cut which is the outgrowth of that past.

In writing of a definite period in truth, but the present the phrase is met years when the grandmothers then living

YE ENTRANCE OF OLD FASHION

contrast to the present "old times" we have in mind. All times, in are old, but wherever with, it refers to the fathers and grandwere young. Ever since there were grandfathers and grandmothers there have been "old times," and these times have kept even pace with the ageing of the world, following, shadow-like, the accumulating years, and always nearly three-quarters of a century behind the present. It therefore follows that the "old times" pictured in this volume have to do with the early part of this century.

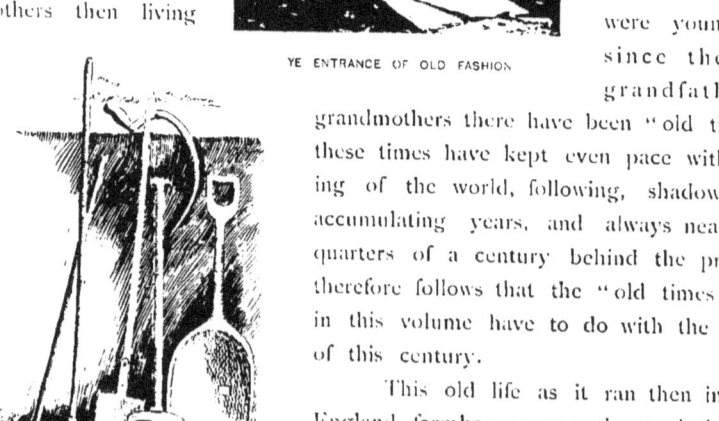

FARM TOOLS

This old life as it ran then in our New England farmhouses was the typical American life, and was not essentially different from country life in any of our Northern States. Even with that of the city it had many things in common. The much the characvillages, and were into the great and stone, now faness may throng noisy streets. Facwith their highgrimy, crowded about, were of the But the century was the Everywhere was

A LOOM

large places had ter of overgrown not yet converted blocks of brick miliar, where business miles and miles of tory towns, too, walled mills and tenements huddling future.
dawn of the new herald of change. activity. The

country was new, and we had many needs which the Old World did not feel. Necessity made us inventors, and ingenuity became an American characteristic. A long line of towns stretched along the Atlantic coast and occupied an occasional interval along the larger streams, and houses were beginning to appear and hamlets to grow farther inland. The adventurous were pushing westward. The heavy canvas-topped wagons drawn by the slow-moving oxen were trundling along the road toward the setting sun. Under the white arch of canvas were stored

FANS AND BACK-COMB

the furniture and household supplies of a family. Behind were driven the sheep and cattle which should form the nucleus of new flocks in the new home.

The century was seven years old before Fulton's steamer made its trial trip.

OLD CHAIRS

Advantage was quickly taken of this new application of power, and soon steam vessels were puffing up and down all the larger rivers and along the coast, though a dozen years elapsed before one ventured across the Atlantic. Railroads were still unthought of. Even wagons were not common for some years after the close of the last century.

There were very few places in the United States whose inhabitants exceeded ten thousand in 1800; but the building of factories shortly commenced, and these became the magnets which drew a great tide of life from the country and from foreign shores into the cities. The factories gave the death-

ONE OF THE OLD HOUSES

blow to the multitude of handicrafts which up to this time had flourished in the New England villages.

The New England town of the period was made up of a group of houses about an open common. At least, it started thus. As the town grew, a second street or a number of them were laid out parallel or at right angles to the first, or houses were erected along the straggling paths which led to the surrounding fields; and the paths in time grew to the dignity of roads, and linked the scattered houses and hamlets to the parent village. The central village, where the lay of the land permitted, was built on a broad hilltop, partly, as in the case of the older towns, for purposes of defence, partly because here the land was less thickly overgrown with trees and underbrush and was more easily cleared. Another reason was that the Old World towns were built thus, and the emigrants to this country naturally did likewise, even though the Old World life in feudal times which gave reason for this was entirely of the past.

Here was the quiet building fronted by weather-worn sheds were parishioners living at a their horses during ser- the tavern, a substantial whose sign swung from a tree or pole close by. four or five little shops lines of comfortable two-

A SILHOUETTE PORTRAIT

meeting-house, a big, the spire. A group of close behind it, where distance might shelter vices. Not far away was and roomy building the front or dangled from Then there would be and stores among the story dwellings.

People in general neglected ornamental trees, though there were before this occasionally persons who had set out shade trees, and places which had started lines of elms along the village streets. About this time Lombardy poplars became fashionable. The poplar was a French tree, and was therefore championed by the Jeffersonian Democrats, who had for France a decided partiality. For the most part these trees have disappeared. Still, here and there their tall, compact, military

A RIVER-BOAT BEFORE THE DAYS OF RAILROADS

forms are seen standing dark and stiff, and with a still lingering air about them of foreign strangeness. The appearance of the common or the village in general was little thought of. Sidewalks received almost no attention, and such paths as there were had been made by the wear of travel.

REELS

What fine buildings those houses of old times were and still are! — not in the least pretentious, but having a certain distinguished air of comfort and stability; no suggestion of the doll-house which so many of our Queen Anne cottages bring to mind, but withal an appearance of quiet and attractive dignity. The supreme effort of the builder seems to have centred in the doorways, which are often quite intricate in their ornament; yet they are never reckless in design, and are always pleasing in effect. Often, too, the decoration of the doorway was echoed in the ornament of the window-frames and the cornice under the eaves. Piazzas were rare, but many houses had a porch before the entrance.

A COMFORTABLE FARMHOUSE

The finer residences had knockers on the front doors. Door-bells came into use a little later. Instead of the modern door-knobs, iron latches were used, or in some cases wooden ones. If the latch had no thumb-piece — and the more primitive ones had not — a string was attached and run through a hole bored for the purpose just above. The latch was on the inside, and there was no way of raising it except the latchstring hung out. Locking was readily accomplished by pulling in the string. Some houses had wooden buttons on the doors just over the latch, which, when turned down, held the latch in

THE FLAX-WHEEL

FEBRUARY

its notch and thus locked the door. In still other cases doors were locked by means of a fork thrust in just above the latch, but for the most part doors of buildings, both public and private, went unlocked

Houses in town, and the meeting-house as well, were painted red or yellow. Many houses, especially those belonging to the poorer people and those outside the main village, were unpainted. On some of our old buildings may yet be seen suggestions of these

KITCHEN UTENSILS

former brilliant hues, though sun and storm have been softening the tones all through the years, so that only a shadowy tint of the old red or yellow still clings to the weather-worn clapboards. Most houses changed color to white, when that became the fashion fifty years ago. Blinds of the modern pattern were not much used before the century was well begun. In the Indian days heavy wooden doors were swung across the window openings to bar the passage, but after 1750 the Indians were no longer objects of terror to New England people.

The larger wild animals were almost altogether gone by this time in the regions longest settled. The sheep pastured on the hills were not now in danger from prowling wolves or bears. Some of the old farmers had perhaps in their

GOURDS AND PIGGINS

younger days heard the dismal cry of the former far off in the woods, perhaps had shot a black bear or two, or caught a few in traps; but now a bear, wolf, or wildcat was rarely seen anywhere in the vicinity of the older towns. Deer had almost disappeared. Wild turkeys could still be shot in considerable numbers, and in the fall great flocks of pigeons made their flights in sufficient numbers to darken the sky.

To the boys, that seems the golden age when the Indians lurked in the deep woods, when bears and wolves and other wild beasts had to be fought with. At such a time who would not be a hero! Hoeing corn, digging potatoes, bringing in wood, milking cows, where is the chance to show our talents in these things? The heroes are in the West, the North, or in the Tropics now. These present times are slow and dull, and hold no such opportunity as had the fathers, for the valiant youth to show his quality. But this feeling is a mistaken one. The lives of the fathers were many times dull to them; they had much monotonous labor; wild animals were nuisances, which caused loss and worry; while the Indians gave them many a scare, and awakened little feeling in the youngster of that day beyond one of terror. At the time of which I write the pioneer epoch

THE LONDON STAGE COACH

was past in New England, but many stories of Indians and wild beasts were told about the firesides on winter evenings.

In a country town the coming of the stage-coach was one of the events of its daily life. Some places were visited by the coaches once or twice a week, others once a day or even oftener. When the lumbering coach swept down the village street with crack of whip and blast of horn, everybody tried to see it as it rumbled past. Happy was the man or boy whom business or pleasure called to the tavern when the driver with a

A MILL-YARD IN THE VALLEY

flourish brought his horses to a standstill before the door. The driver was a very important person in the eyes of most of the villagers, and by none was his importance more highly appreciated than by himself. His dignity was made the more impressive by the high beaver hat he wore. News was slow in travelling, and the papers of the day were rather barren of the gossipy items which the average human being craves. This man of the world, therefore, who, in his journeyings, saw and heard so much of which his fellowmen were ignorant, assumed a magnified importance. He always found ready listeners, and his opinions had much weight. If inclined to be reticent he was questioned and coaxed to divulge his knowledge of the happenings in the outside world with no little anxiety. When railroads came, the coaches travelled remoter ways. Some found a last resting-place in backyards, and there amid other rubbish, grasses, and weeds gradually fell to pieces. Others,

A SUNNY GLEN

A QUIET DAY

may be that some of the old New England coaches are still at work in those rugged regions.

Another characteristic vehicle of the times was a long, heavy wagon with an arched canvas top and high board sides, drawn by from four to ten horses, which travelled between Boston and towns inland, conveying tea, coffee, and store goods, and returning with a load of pork, butter, cheese, and grain. These wagons were useful when families wished to travel long distances. When the railroads began to do their former work the wagons were utilized by the emigrants, and finally on the Western plains were given the name of "prairie schooners."

When an inland town was in the neighborhood of a navigable stream the heavier supplies, such as sugar, rum, and molasses, were brought up the river in big flat-boats. These boats were clumsy, square-ended affairs, with a narrow cabin across the stern just high enough for a man to stand up in, where were a couple of bunks and a rude stove. A big, square sail on a thirty-foot mast moved the craft, but when the wind failed it was necessary to resort to poling. The helmsman had his post on the roof of the cabin, and he with one other man made up the crew. Sometimes they ate their meals on board, sometimes stopped at a village on the banks and went to the tavern. When darkness settled down they hitched somewhere along shore, but at times, when the wind was fair and the moon bright, would sail on all night.

Post-offices were in the early days far less common than now, and postage was expensive, varying in amount with the distance the missive travelled. Letters were not stamped, but the sum charged was marked on the corner and collected by the postmaster on delivery. Envelopes were not in common use till about 1850. Letters were usually written on large-

A BARN-DOOR GROUP

sized paper, and as much as possible crowded on a sheet. The sheet was dexterously folded so that the only blank space, purposely so left, made the front and back of the missive. Then the letter was directed and sealed with wax, and was ready for the mail. Towns not favored with a post-

A TURN IN THE ROAD

office would get their mail by the stage-coach, or, if off the stage routes, would send a post-rider periodically to the nearest office. As the post-rider came jogging back with his saddle-bags full of newspapers and letters, the

A NEW ENGLAND VALLEY

sound of his horn which told of his approach was a very pleasant one to those within the farm-houses, who always looked forward with eagerness to the day which brought the county paper with the news.

The out-door farm life of that time was distinguished by its long hours and the amount of muscle required. The tools were rude and clumsy, and the machines which did away with hand labor were very few. From seed-time to harvest, work began with the coming of daylight in the morning, and only ceased when in the evening the gray gloom of night began to settle down.

Up to this time little fencing had been done about the pasture land, that being common property on which everybody turned loose their sheep and cattle. Many of the creatures wore bells, which tinkled and jingled on the hillsides and in the woods from morn till night. But now the towns were dividing the "commons" among the property-holders, fences were

A HILLTOP VILLAGE

built, and the flocks separated. On rocky land many stone walls were built, but in the lowlands the usual fence was made by digging a ditch, and on the ridge made by the earth thrown out making a low barrier of rails, stakes, and brush. Gradually more substantial fences were built, for the most part of the zigzag Virginia rail pattern.

Oxen did most of the heavy farm-work, such as ploughing and hauling, and it was not till after 1825 that horses became more general. The common cart which then answered in the place of our two-horse wagon was a huge two-wheeled affair having usually a heavy box body on the "ex." But when used in haying, the sides of the box were removed and long stakes were substituted.

In the summer the men were out before sun up, swinging their scythes through the dewy grass, and leaving long, wet windrows behind them for the boys to spread. Mowing, turning, and raking were all done by hand, which made the labor of haying an extended one. In the busiest times the women and girls of the family often helped in the fields "tending" hay, or loading it, or raking after. They helped, too, in harvesting the grain and flax, and later in picking up apples in the orchard. They did the milking

A LITTLE LAKE

the year round, using clumsy wooden pails, and for a seat, a heavy three-legged stool or a block of wood. The smaller children drove the cows to pasture in the morning and brought them back at night, often a distance of a mile or two along lonesome roadways or by-paths.

When the grain ripened, it was reaped by hand with the slender, saw-edged sickles. The peas and oats, which were sowed together, had to be mowed and gotten in; the flax had to be pulled and rotted; there was hoeing to be done, and the summer was full of work. In the fall the corn had to be cut and husked and the stalks brought in, the pumpkins and squashes gathered, potatoes dug, the haying finished, and the apples picked. Most farms had large orchards about them, and many barrels of apples were stowed away in the cellar, but the larger part was made into cider. There would usually be several little cider-mills in a town, whose creaking machinery could be heard on many a cool autumn day groaning under its labors. The shaking of the apple-trees and carting the fruit to mill, and the taking

THE NEW ENGLAND COUNTRY

copious draughts of the sweet liquid through a straw from the tub that received it from the press, and then the return with the full barrels — all this had more of the frolic in it than real work, particularly for the boys. The sweet apples, in large part, were run through the mill by themselves, and the cider was boiled down at home into a thick fluid known as apple-molasses, used for sweetening pies, sauce, and puddings. When harvesting was done, the cellar was full of vegetables in barrels and bins and heaps, and heavy casks of cider lined the walls, and little space was left for passageways. Even in broad daylight it was a place mysterious, gloomy, and dungeon-like; yet its very fulness which made it thus was suggestive of good cheer.

Winter, too, brought plenty of work, but it was not so arduous and long-continued as that of summer. There was the stock to feed and water

A VILLAGE SCENE

and keep comfortable; the threshing to do; trees must be felled in the woods and sledded to the home yard, there to be worked up into fireplace length; tools needed mending; there was the flax to attend to, and, if new fencing was to be done in the spring, rails must be split.

Grain was threshed out with hand-flails on the barn floor. On many days of early winter and from many a group of farm buildings the rhythmic beat of the flails sounded clear on the frosty air as straw and grain parted company. When it was necessary to go to mill, the farmer filled a couple of bags, fastened them across the back of his horse, mounted in front, and trotted off to get it ground, or perhaps his wife or one of the children mounted instead and did the errand. The grist-mill was in some hollow where the water paused above in a sleepy pond, and then, having turned the

SNOW-FIELDS ON THE HILLS

great slow-revolving wooden wheel against the side of the mill, tumbled noisily on down the ravine.

In the earliest days of spring, if the farm had a maple orchard within its borders, there were trees to tap, and sap to gather and boil down. The snow still lay deep in the woods where the maples grew, and the sap-gathering was done with an ox-sled on which was set a huge cask. In some sheltered nook of the woods a big kettle was swung over an open-air fire, and the boiling-down process commenced.

Not much farm produce was sold for money; the people raised and made much more of what they ate and wore than at present, and exchanged with neighbors and the village storekeeper whatever they had a surplus of

MARCH

for things which they lacked. Even the minister and doctor were paid in part with wood, grain, and other produce. At the beginning of the century accounts were kept in pounds, shillings, and pence, and the money in use was of foreign coinage, mainly English and Spanish.

The kitchen was the centre of family life. Here a vast amount of work was done. Here they ate, spent their evenings, and commonly received visitors. Often it served as a sleeping-room besides. Its size was ample, though the ceiling was low and pretty sure to be crossed by a ponderous beam of the framework of the house, the lower half projecting from the plastering above. A few straight-backed chairs sat stiffly up against the wainscoted wall, and seemed to have an air of reserve that would change to surprise if one ventured to move or use them. There stood the dresser,

CLEARED LAND

with bright array of pewter, a small table, a bed turned up against the wall and hidden by curtains, a cradle, a stand, a great high-backed settle, and lastly, extending almost across one end of the room, was the most important feature of the kitchen, the fireplace.

Let us take an early morning look into one of these old kitchens. Dusky shadows still linger; we cannot make objects out clearly; one or two coals are glowing in the cavernous mouth of the fireplace, and a wisp of smoke steals upward and is lost in the gloomy chimney. It is late in the fall. When winter really sets in, the turned-up bed will come into use. Somebody is moving about in the bedroom, and now the door is opened and the man of the house, in frowzled head, comes from the sleeping-room. He is in his shirt-sleeves, and the heels of his big slippers clatter on the floor as he shuffles across to the fireplace. He is a smooth-faced, middle-aged

GATHERING SAP IN THE SUGAR ORCHARD

man, vigorous, but slow-moving, and bent by hard work. He pokes away the ashes, throws on the coals a few sticks from a pile of three-foot wood on the floor close by, and in a few moments there is a fine blaze and crackle. The room is chilly, and the man rubs his hands together, stooping forward to catch the warmth from the fire. A scratching is heard on the outside door. He shuffles over and opens it. The cat glides in and rubs against him gratefully as she goes over to the fireplace, where she seats herself on the hearth and proceeds to make an elaborate toilet.

The man kicks off his slippers and pulls on a pair of stiff, heavy boots. He takes his coat from a peg by the fireplace, puts it on and his cap, and goes out. Every footstep falls clear and distinct on the frozen ground.

THE NEW ENGLAND COUNTRY

The big arm of the well-sweep in the yard creaks as he lowers the bucket for water. Soon he returns with a brimming pail, fills the iron tea-kettle, then goes out again.

The kettle, suspended from the crane, seems quite shocked by this deluge of cold water. It swings in nervous motion on its pot-hook and shakes

WAYSIDE BERRY-PICKERS

from its black sides the water-drops, which fall with a quick hiss of protest into the fire. The heat below waxes greater, and the cat moves to a cooler position.

It is lighter now. The tea-kettle recovers from its ill-humor, and, half asleep, sings through its nose a droning song of contentment and sends up the chimney quite a little cloud of steam. Now the woman of the family has appeared and bustles about getting breakfast. She calls the children at the chamber door. Down they come, and crowd about the fire or scrub themselves in the wash-basin on the table. Grandfather is up, and he and the older boys go out-doors. Grandma helps the smaller children fasten their clothes and wash their faces, and assists about the housework.

Some of the older girls, perhaps grandma or the mother also, soon take their wooden pails and go to the barn to milk the cows. When they returned,

A FARM AMID THE BIG HILLS

they strained the milk through cloths held over the tops of the pails into the brown earthen pans, and then were ready to help with the breakfast preparations. A second kettle has been hung from the crane, in which potatoes are boiling. Coals have been raked out on the hearth, and over them is set a long-legged spider on which slices of pork are sizzling.

By the time breakfast was ready, the men, by reason of their open-air exercise, had appetites which nought but very hearty food could appease. Before they sat down to eat, the family gathered about the table and stood while the head of the family asked a blessing. Then the older ones seated themselves, while the children went to a small second table at one side, about which they stood and ate, trotting over to the main table when they wished to replenish their plates.

Many families had cider on the table to drink at every meal. Other people would sometimes tea, ter was not cept for com- er to such an present. Coffee with molasses so accustomed come to this, have coffee or though the lat- much used ex- pany, and neith- extent as at was sweetened ordinarily, and did palates be- that when sugar came into more general use, it was considered by many a very poor substitute.

A LITTLE HOUSE ON THE HILLSIDE

Breakfast eaten, the household gathered about the main table once more and stood while thanks were returned. Then followed family worship. It was customary to read the Bible from beginning to end,—a chapter each morning,—all the family reading verses in turn; and then, if they were musical, a hymn was sung. Lastly, all knelt while prayer was offered.

A STREAM FROM THE HILLS

Work now began again. The men left to take up their labor out of doors, while the women busied themselves in the house with their varied tasks. As the morning wore away, preparation began for dinner. What was known as a "boiled dinner" was most often planned. It was prepared in a single great pot. First the meat was put in; then from time to time, according as the particular things were quick or slow in cooking, the vegetables were added, — potatoes, beets, squash, turnip, and cabbage, — and probably in the same pot a bag of Indian pudding. When clock or noon-mark registered twelve, the dinner was dished up and the men called in. The meal was hearty and simple, and the family did not feel the need of much besides the meat and vegetables. Even bread was hardly thought necessary. Sometimes pie or pudding was brought on for dessert, but not regularly. The pie-eating era began a generation later.

At six o'clock the supper-table was set. The cows had been fed and milked; the boys had brought in the wood, and as they had no wood-boxes,

A SAW-MILL

they dumped the heavy three-foot sticks on the floor by the fire, or stood it up on end against the wall at one side, or piled it between the legs of the kitchen table; and other odd jobs were done, and the family gathered about the table. Bread and milk was quite apt to be the chief supper dish.

After the blessing was asked and the elders had seated themselves, the children would fill their pewter porringers or wooden bowls and pull their chairs up about the fireplace. Instead, they would sometimes crouch on the stone hearth, while the fire glowed and crackled and set the lights and shadows playing about the little figures. Their chatter back and forth and the company of the fire made their circle like a little world in itself, and the grown folks and their talk seemed far, far away.

When supper was ended and the dishes done, the women took up their sewing and knitting. Almost everything worn was of home manufacture, and the task of making and mending was a never-ending one. Even the little girls of four or five years were not idle, but were taking their first lessons with the knitting-needles. The men had less real work to do,— perhaps were occupied with mending a broken harness or

A SPRING MORNING

tool, making a birch broom, whittling out a few clothes-pins, or constructing a box-trap in which to catch mice. Sometimes certain of the family played games. Evening, too, was a time for reading.

Just before the children went to bed, the family laid aside all tasks and games, and read a chapter from the Bible and had prayers. By nine o'clock all had retired except the father,— the head of the family,— who wound the clock, pulled off his boots in a boot-jack of his own making, and yawned as he shovelled the ashes over some of the larger hard-wood coals, lest the fire should be lost during the night. Then he, too, disappeared, and the fire snapped more feebly, with now and then a fresh but short-lived effort to blaze, and so faded into a dull glow and left the gloomy shadows of the room in almost full sway.

It is difficult to compare the old life with the new and say that in any particular way one was better than the other, and decide under which conditions character would grow most manly or most womanly. Human nature is the same now as fifty or seventy-five years ago; but that nature grows in a different soil, and surrounded by a different atmosphere. Our present standards are unlike the old, the conditions surrounding us have changed, and the way in which our feelings, our desires, and aspirations find expression is changed as well.

It is certain that all the elements of life and growth are within easier

A WILLOW-LINED RIVER

reach, and may more easily be drawn together and assimilated, that under favorable conditions one can get a finer and broader culture. Nature with all its forces, holding power for help and hindrance, has been brought more under man's subjection. Contributions to the sum of human thought and knowledge have been many and valuable. As the years have slipped away the upward path has been made broader and smoother, and one can travel it in more comfort and go much faster. But, at the same time, the downward paths have increased in number and attractiveness, and the narrower ways and more rigid training of three generations ago would unquestionably have held some steady who now are deteriorating.

The fathers made the path toward virtue both narrow and rugged. It required sturdy self-control to keep that way; but each sternly held himself, his family, and his neighbors to the task. Any backsliding or stepping aside called for severe reprimand or punishment. About their lives was a certain forbidding formality and setness. They had a powerful sense

APRIL — ONE OF THE OLD VILLAGE STREETS

of independence, but were very conservative. Any change of thought or action was looked upon as dangerous, and they often made what was their independence another's bonds. Life was to them very serious. In it, according to their interpretation, there was room for little else than sober years of work. What enjoyment they got in life came from the satisfaction in work accomplished, in an improved property, and in prosperous sons and daughters.

Men's character moulds their features. It graved deep lines of stubborn firmness on the faces of the men of that time. There were shown determination and enterprise and ingenuity. In the eyes were steadiness and sturdy honesty. But the softening which the free play of humor and imagination would help produce were lacking. The man's nature was petrified

A LOOK DOWN ON THE CONNECTICUT

into a rock which held its own, and withstood the sunshine and the buffeting storm with equal firmness. He had ability and willingness to bear great burdens, and the generation did a vast amount of work in the world.

The individual to-day is much more independent of the world close about him than he was seventy-five years ago. He asks less of his neighbors, they less of him. The interests of the community are of less importance to him, and he is of less importance to the community. The town which in the old days would have been a little world to him is now but a small space on the earth. Man has grown more restless. A quiet life of simple usefulness is not enough. His fingers itch for money and he dreams of fame. He feels the swirl of the current which draws him toward those great whirlpools of life, — our modern cities. There alone, it seems to him, are things done on a grand scale to be admired; there alone he sees fair scope for energy and ability. One by one the country dwellers leave the home farms, and some there are win fame and some get fortune, but many are forever lost sight of.

THE SPRING HOEING

In times past there was less hurry and more content. To be satisfied has is to have happiness, whether one lives in a hovel or in a mansion. To live with economy in comfort was once enough. But the view of what constitute the necessities of comfort has changed vastly, and what would once have been accounted luxury may now be but a painful meagreness. The people formerly travelled very little, and had small contact with outside life, save that of neighboring towns, which differed little from that at home. Journeys which now, with the aid of steam, are slight undertakings, were then very serious. In the case of journeys of any length, prayers were offered in church for the traveller's safe return; and when the journey was ended, the minister gave thanks for the happy accomplishment of the trip. The labor and uncertainty connected with a long journey, and the unfamiliarity with the destination, made home seem a very safe and comfortable place. The newspapers were prosy and slow, and gave little account of the outside world to excite and attract the young. Long reports of legislative and congressional doings, and discussions of subjects political and religious, filled many columns. No space was wasted on

light reading. The object was not so much to interest as to instruct the reader. The communications and reports of news were inclined to be prosy and pompous, but were always thoughtful and courteous, rarely abusive or trivial. There was an almost entire lack of local news, and such things as stories, slang, or nonsense were not allowed.

PART II

THE NEW ENGLAND OF TO-DAY

THE FRIENDLY GUIDE

THE New England country has with the ageing of the century been depopulated. The causes are various, but the evolution of the newspaper has much to do with this. Visions of movement, and wealth, and fame penetrate daily to the smallest village. Youth has always elements of unfixity and uneasiness. It craves stir and excitement. The future is full of golden possibilities. Riches or position present no height which may not be scaled. But it is not the farm which holds these higher possibilities. No, they are to be won in store, or shop, or bank, where the noisy tides of the big towns keep up their restless sway through the leagues of brick-walled city streets. In the city is always movement. Not a paper comes into the country village but that tells of some grand emprise, some fresh

A HILL TOWN

excitement, that has its home in a familiar near city. But the chronicler for the home village finds no items more worthy of note than that some one's cow has died, and that Amanda Jones is visiting Susan Smith. The contrast presented is one of home monotony and triviality, and city stir and grandeur.

THE BACK DOOR

The picture is not altogether a true one. Acquaintance with the big places is to the country boy almost uniformly disappointing. The buildings are not so high nor so fine as he supposed. The din and crowds of the city streets grow confusing and wearisome. If he stays and gains a situation, and begins to work his way up in the world, he finds competition intense, his freedom sharply curtailed, and his lodgings narrow and in many ways lacking comfort. If he lives on his wages, which at first will be very small, close economy is required in food, clothes, and other expenses. In summer the heat is apt to make office and lodging-place stiflingly disagreeable. All through the year memories of the home farm, if he be imaginatively inclined, make Arcadian pictures in his mind, and he many times questions if he has not jumped from the frying-pan into the fire.

No one place holds every element of pleasure or comfort. The country has its lacks, so has the city. The ideal home is perhaps in the country village within easy travelling distance of some big town. Thus you may largely avoid the drawbacks of either place, while you have within reach all their pleasures. To live far back among the hills, cut off from the nearest railway station by many miles of hard travelling, is, in these modern days, a positive hardship. Few young people will settle down contentedly where they are so cut off from the pleasures of seeing the world by occasional railroad trips, and getting the glimpses they crave of the busier life of the cities. Hence the tide sets away from the remoter towns. The masses always follow the turn of the current whichever way it shows strong tendency to run, and the boys, as they grow up, live in full expectation of leaving the home place after school-days are over. One by one they go from the valleys and the hill-tops, and merge into the busier life of the factory villages and the cities. An air of depression lingers over the regions they leave. The most vigorous life has departed, enterprise is asleep, thrift lags. There are still houses neatly kept, with clean, well-tilled fields about, and a town now and then which is a happy exception to the rule; but there is much which is hopeless and despondent. Few roads can be followed far without coming

WINTER TWILIGHT — GOING UP FOR ONE MORE SLIDE

upon some broken-windowed ruin of a house, now for years unoccupied, and wholly given over to decay. The children left, drawn by dreams of the gains the city or the sea or the far West offered; and the parents are gone, too, now. The shingles and clapboards loosen and the roof sags, and within, damp, mossy decay has fastened itself to walls, floor, and ceiling of every room. Gaps have broken in the stone walls along the roadway, and the brambles are thick springing on either side. In the front yard is a gnarled, untrimmed apple-tree with a great broken limb sagging to the ground, and about a ragged growth of bushes. As time goes on, the house falls piece by piece, and at last only the shattered chimney stands, a grim monument of the one-day comfortable home — a memorial of the dead past.

Yet even now life is not all of the past. Amidst the rubbish careful watching might reveal many of the little creatures of the field, and at eventide of summer days you might see a darting of wings and descry a little company of swallows dipping toward the chimney's open cavern.

Some of the deserted homes would be still habitable, and that very comfortably so, were there tenants. The life possible on these farms would seem much happier and more desirable than that possible to the poor family in the tenement of a factory village or in the crowded quarters of our cities. But the country is to such very "lonesome," and there is hardly a city family of the more ignorant classes but will choose squalor in the city rather than comfort in the country. The noise and continual movement of the town have become a part of their lives, and severed from that it is but a blank, unspeaking landscape unfolds before their eyes. Nature is really never lonesome. Only our habit and education make it so seem. Nature is always singing, whether in our fellow humans, or in the hills and valleys, or in the life of plants and animals. It is we lack eyes to see and ears to hear. Nevertheless, mankind is naturally social, and though Robinson

A HILL-TOWN VILLAGE

Crusoe and his island were very interesting, we do not envy him the experience, and demand at least a few congenial neighbors within easy reach.

HOUSES AND OUT-BUILDINGS BY THE WAYSIDE

There is hardly any purely farming community in New England but that has decreased in population within the past fifty years. It has been the hill towns which have suffered most, but the valley towns have been affected as well. It has become the habit to account all country life dull, and the city's superior liveliness, and the chances to earn ready money offered by stores and factories, draw away the life of even the most favored communities. New England is to day much less a region of thrifty Yankee farmers than it is a land of busy manufacturing villages. Of these, enterprise and ingenious inventiveness are characteristic. They call to them a large foreign population which fills the monotonous rows of tenements in the neighborhood of the mills, or in the case of the more thrifty establishes itself in little separate family homes on the outskirts. The farming regions about naturally take to market gardening, and these places become the chief buyers of produce for the country miles about.

Farming towns within easy distance of the railroads usually attain a fair prosperity, and energy and forethought give good returns for labor expended. The towns themselves with their elm-shadowed streets are neatly kept, and there is a certain pride taken in the good appearance of the homes half hidden in the drooping foliage. In the remoter towns are found thrifty dairy farms here and there, but the villages as a whole are inclined to look weatherworn and hopeless. Many of the houses have been strangers to fresh paint for a score of years or more; and others, though still inhabited, depress with their broken chimnies, leaky roofs, and decrepit out-buildings; while there are not wanting the homes altogether deserted, silent, broken-windowed, and sepulchral. Often these upland towns are nearly barren of

NEW ENGLAND ROCKS

well-grown trees which might add so much to their appearance, and the trees there are, look wind-blown and storm-beaten. This, with the thin, weedy grasses which grow on the opens before the churches, gives such places an accumulated forlornness.

It may be possible to find one of the outlying hamlets entirely deserted. There are little villages where you may find half a dozen or more forsaken homes, and no more than one or two still occupied; and the whole village and land is concentrated in one or two big farms,—big only in acres, however. There is slight attempt, as a rule, to keep up a thorough tillage. The best of the fields are gone over each year and a scanty harvest gleaned, and it may be questioned if equal labor on fewer acres would not produce greater results. The surplus buildings of the now depopulated village receive slight care, and time and decay deal hardly with them. The

HOLDING THE HORSES WHILE HIS FATHER GOES IN TO GET A DRINK OF WATER

best of them serve as storage places for farm crops or tools. The more broken-down are levied upon occasionally for a few boards to mend a fence or a leak in one of the neighboring buildings, and so is hastened their time of complete ruin.

Some places have won the favor of the summer visitors, and so have gained renewed prosperity. A few weeks' sojourn far from the heat and noise of the city on these quiet, breezy hill-tops is no small pleasure, and many a person of means takes pride in the cottage home he has bought in some nook he thinks especially favored by nature, and looks forward all through the lengthening days of the spring to the time when he can unlock its door once more, wind the clock in the hall, and settle himself with his

family for the yearly vacation. He finds not a little fussing and fixing to employ him about the place, and he saunters forth in his oldest suit, when the notion takes him, to talk with his neighbors the farmers. The chances are he gets off his coat and renews his youth by helping in the hay-field, and there, like enough, the rest of his flock hunt him out, and all have a

AT THE RAILROAD STATION

the tinkling murmur of the waterfalls sounded in his ear a call to get forth his fishing-rod. He was not long settled in his vacation home before the fishing-tackle was forthcoming, and he might be seen with vast caution and seriousness following up the neighboring brook through the tangled woods, and across the pastures among the rank-growing ferns and grasses, casting the fly and trailing it after the most approved fashion along the surface of the water, and perchance, if destiny favored, pulling forth at times a dainty little trout. The streams are so thoroughly fished that at finger-length, in the more accessible regions, the fish is esteemed a prize. Driving is always in order. There are glens, and waterfalls, and high hills with wonderfully far outlooks, and delightful winding valleys, to visit almost without number.

On Sunday the summer visitor goes to the village church. Perhaps the services are not as brilliant as those to which he is used, but there is a comfortable simplicity to the place, the people, the sermon, and the singing which charms. The visitor is often a ready and valued helper in making the church and its belongings more attractive, and takes an interest in the schools and library and appearance of the town, which to many a place has been of great assistance. The vacation which includes, beside the ordinary outdoor pleasuring, some of this sort of helpfulness gives a multiplied satisfaction at its close.

The country dwellers of New England are not to-day, in the mass, as strong charactered and vigorously intelligent as were those of the early part of the century. Those elements have found greater attraction and greater chance of reward elsewhere. It often happens that thrift seems to dwell rather with recent comers from across the water than with the older families.

THE RAILWAY-CROSSING — THE VILLAGE

This is sometimes claimed to be because the first will live more meanly than the latter could bring themselves to. The truth is, the new-comers have no pride of family name to sustain, they know attainment rests only on hard work, and their secret of success lies more in their steady labor and good business habits than in any meanness of living. The scions of the old families are looser in their methods and more reckless and showy, and far less given to vigorous work. They may be heard to bewail over this foreign element as usurpers; but in reality comers of thrift and intelligence, whatever their former homes, are a help to the town life. Hard work, saving habits, and the aspiration to give the children of the family an education, has a healthful effect on character, and win oftentimes for those growing up in these homes culture and practical ability equalling the best of that of the older families. If a

A STONE BRIDGE

foreign family takes up with some little house on the outskirts, it may live very shabbily for the first few years. But the land about is gradually brought under full and thrifty tillage, little sheds begin to spring up behind the house, by and by a barn is built, and then the house is made over and an L added, and the progress toward prosperity as presented to the eye is a thing to be admired. It is almost always the remnants of the worn out Yankee families which come on the town, and not these foreigners.

"Yankee" has become almost a synonym for ingeniousness, thrift, and "cuteness." You can't scare him; get him in a tight place and he will

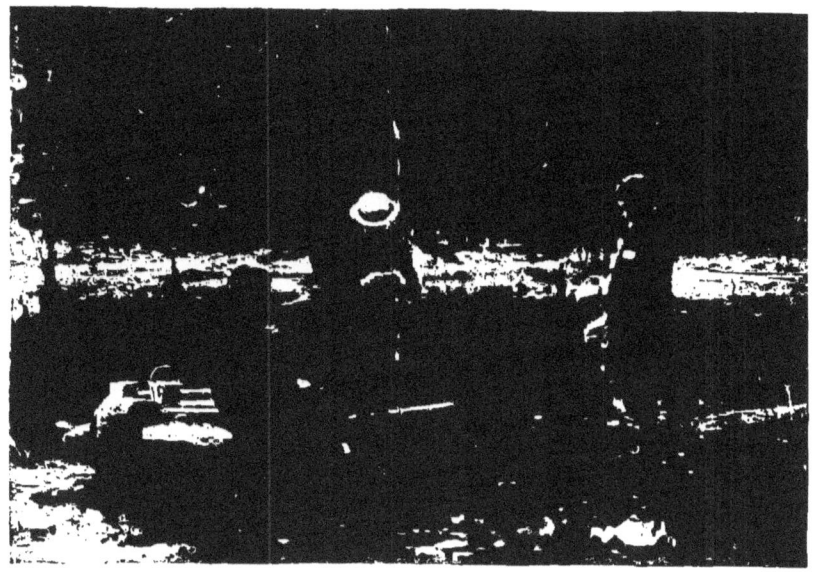

A GROUP OF LITTLE FISHERMEN

find a way out; set him a task and he will find some way to do it in half the time you expected; make him the butt of a joke and he will get even with you and pay heavy interest; no matter what part of the earth you transplant him to or the conditions you surround him with, he accommodates himself to the new circumstances, and proceeds with alacrity to financially profit by them. He is a born arguer, and a born pedler, and a born whittler, a Jack-at-all-trades and good at them all.

This, it may be, is the typical Yankee, and without a doubt such can be found; but not every inhabitant of New England is made that way. Yankees are of all kinds, and the abilities, virtues, and short-comings are much mixed in the parcelling out. The Yankee is a man of opinions, and shows great readiness to impart them to others; but the depth or shallowness of these depends on the man. He is inclined to slow speaking and nasal tones, and when a question is asked has a way of turning it over in his mind once or twice before he gives answer, often improving the interval to spit seriously and meditatively. In bargaining, whatever the amount involved, he is given to dickering, crying down, or upholding the price, according as he is buyer or seller. The thrifty man is sometimes simply the man of push and ability, sometimes the miserly man who drives sharp bargains

A WAYSIDE WATERING-TROUGH

and forecloses mortgages when his poor neighbors are in trouble, and sells hard cider to the drinkers; or he may be one of high standing in church and community, who, though stickling for fairness, is sure to buy low and sell high; who is up at sunrise in summer and long before daylight in winter; who makes long days and fills them with hard work, and is esteemed a hard master by sons and hired men; who lives frugally, and when it comes to spending, as the saying goes, "squeezes the dollar until the eagle squeals."

As a rule New England country people save nothing above expenses, and even then, spending all they earn, can have few more than the most common comforts of life, and rarely a luxury. Circumstance or some untoward accident of fate may bring this result, but an unstriving lack of thrift is more frequently the cause. Those of this class have a way of being always a little behind in what they do, and there is a dragging want

A COUNTRY SCHOOL WATCHING A TRAIN GO BY

of vitality in what they attempt. They are a little late in planting, a little late in harvesting. They never get full crops, and fall below the best always in quality, and are apt to suffer loss through frost or foul weather. "The stitch in time which saves nine" about their buildings they

AN OLD BURYING-GROUND

do not take, and these buildings lose boards here and there, and presently begin to sag and need a prop to keep them from coming down prone. So crops, and animals, and farm-tools are ill-protected, and there is increased loss.

As compared with the typical Southerner, the Yankee has less warmth of enthusiasm, less open-heartedness and chivalry, but he is steadier and has greater staying-power. The ne'er-do-well class of the North may wear their hearts on their sleeves and be as free as air in their kindliness and generosity, but Yankee thrift, however generous or philanthropic, is self-controlled and inclined to be reticent and politic. But though this may lessen the charm and poetry of it, there is no doubting its increased effectiveness.

Thrift is apt to become with the well-to-do a sort of passion. The lack of it in a neighbor stirs continued and sarcastic criticism. On the other hand, thrift easily runs into closeness; but the worshipper of thrift is not mean and entirely selfish in this regard. It is a pleasure to him to see well-tilled fields, even if they belong to others, and he has the wish to make what attracts him general. The rich at their death often leave their fortunes in whole or in part to some charity or educational institution which will further a more general thrift.

In stories of New England village-life we find a curious dialect used by the characters. Quaintness and uncouthness are both prominent. To

one thoroughly acquainted with its people these stories savor of exaggeration and caricature. Ignorance everywhere uses bad grammar, whether in town or country, New England or elsewhere. Isolation tends also to careless speech. But the New Englander has not either, as a rule, to so marked a degree as to make him the odd specimen of humanity pictured in books. Life in the small villages and on the outlying farms does not present very numerous social advantages, and the result is a necessity for depending on one's own resources. This, with those possessed of some mental vigor, develops individuality of thought and stable and forceful character. In the towns it requires the consultation and help of about half a dozen friends for a young

A MASSACHUSETTS MOUNTAIN.

person to accomplish any given object, great or small. On the farm, where neighbors are few, the boy or girl does his or her own thinking and working. Such have more pith and point to their brain movement, and in after life under as favoring circumstances will accomplish more.

THE FERRYBOAT.

Individuality expresses itself in manner and speech as well as thought and odd ways and queer ideas and peculiar observations are to be met with very commonly in the New England country. The heavy work brings a certain amount of clumsiness with the strength. The rough clothes usually worn, and the slight care given them, often make an individual grotesque,

FALL ON THE CONNECTICUT

and the majority of the workers attain to the picturesque in their costumes with their variety of patched and faded oldness. A peculiarity of recent years has come with the fashion of derby hats. There is a naturalness about an old slouch hat, however ancient, stained, and misshapen. If it does not grow old gracefully, it at least does so logically and without reminding the beholder of a more exalted past. But the battered and leaky derby retains to the last a stiff look of aristocracy which ill fits its dilapidated seediness.

But whether a man is uncouth or not depends on other things than his occupation. Neatness is a growth from within rather than from without, and though no sensible farmer works in his Sunday clothes on week-days,

JUNE

THE NEW ENGLAND COUNTRY

there are many by whom you are agreeably impressed, no matter where you meet them. A look from the car window on a rainy day, as you pause at the villages on your route, reveals a curious motley group hanging about the platform. The depot is a favorite resort on stormy days when work is slack on the farm; but loafing is not characteristic of the best of the community, and it is hardly fair to judge all by the specimens who here present themselves.

Indoors, where presides the housewife, we expect to find neatness in supreme rule, for the New England woman has in that a wide repute. It is to be doubted if the old-time shining and spotless interiors which the grandmothers tell about are as universal now as formerly. But house-cleanings come with great regularity in most families, and the consumption of brooms and scrubbing-brushes in New England is something enormous. With the advent of wall-paper and carpets and the great variety of furniture and knick-knacks now within reach, has come a discontent with the old simplicity, and the changes are often not pleasing. Taste runs too much in wall-paper and carpets to dark colors and pronounced patterns, and the rooms appear boxy. If much money is spent on furniture it is apt to be spent on style rather than on substantial and quiet comfort. The pictures on the walls are usually a queer collection, from — it would be hard to imagine where; of colored prints, engravings cut from newspapers, and photographs of deceased

members of the family. The science of house decoration is something very modern, and it will take time to learn how to do it simply and harmoniously.

Life's currents pursue a tangled course, and while we catch many strains of harmony, there are discordant notes of which we rarely get entirely out of hearing. New England is not perfect, but once to have known is always

THE ACADEMY

to love it, no matter how far one wanders or how fair new regions open before one's eyes. Its changing seasons, its rugged hills and tumbling streams, its winding roadways, its villages and little farms, cling in the memory and sing siren songs of enticement. Nature is sometimes harsh, but she has many moods, and nowhere more than here; and if harsh sometimes, she is at other times exceeding sweet. In cold or heat, storm or sunshine, New England's rough fields are still the true Arcadia to her sons and daughters.

PART III

NEW ENGLAND AS THE TRAVELLER SEES IT

TO really see and know New England one must leave the railroads and take time for a long tramp or drive. Railroads are only intended to link together the cities and larger towns, and they seek the level and monotonous for their routes, and pursue always as straight and prosaic a course as circumstances will admit. The view from the windows of ragged banks of earth or rock, where a path has been cut through a hill, or of the sandy embankments, where a hollow has been filled, and of pastures, swamps, and stumpy, brushy acres, where the timber has lately been cut off, are often dismal. At the same time the real country as seen from the winding, irregular roadways that link the villages and scattered farms together may be quite cheerful and pleasing.

A HORSE-CHESTNUT MAN

With the purpose of seeing the real New England in its highways and byways, its hills and valleys, its nooks and corners, I started out one autumn day on a buckboard. I had a little bay horse, fat and good-natured, quite content to stop as often and long as I chose, and to busy herself nibbling the grass and bushes by the roadside, while I sketched or photographed. She had a decided disinclination for fast travelling, and wanted to walk

AFTERGLOW

THE VILLAGE CHURCH

It was nine o'clock when I left Old Hadley in Central Massachusetts and turned northward up the valley. A cold wind was blowing, and many gray cloud-masses were sailing overhead. The region about was one of the fairest in New England,—a wide, fertile valley basin stretching twenty miles in either direction. The Connecticut River loops through it with many graceful curves, and blue ranges of hills bound it on every side. At intervals of about ten miles on this level you come upon the few scores of houses, which cluster about the churches at the centre of the towns, and there are many little hamlets where are lesser groups of homes.

I was jogging across some meadows, when I came to a few houses flanked by numerous out-buildings and half hidden by the trees about them. Some children were by the roadside. They had rakes and a big basket, and were intent on gathering the maple leaves which carpeted the ground. They stopped to watch me as I approached.

"Take my picture,"

ONE OF THE HUMBLER HOUSES

cried a stout little girl, and then threw the basket over her head and struck an attitude.

"All right," was my reply.

"Oh!" she said, "I want my cat in," and raced off to the house to secure it.

She was no sooner back and in position than she found a new trouble. She had on a little cap with a very narrow visor, and as the sun had now come out, its bright light made her eyes wink. Suddenly she spoke up and said the little cap made her cry, and wanted to get a hat, if I would let her. When she returned I made haste to snap the camera before any other ideas could occur to her. We were pretty well acquainted by the time I finished, and she wanted to know how much I charged for my picture, and said she guessed she would get one if I came that way again.

The town of Sunderland lay a little beyond. It is a typical valley town, with a long, wide street lined by elms and maples, thickset on either side by the white

A DESERTED HOME

houses of its people. Everything looked thrifty and well kept. The wind blew gustily, and sometimes would start the leaves which had just begun to strew the ground beneath and send windrows of them scurrying along the road like live armies on a charge.

I was in the village in the late afternoon, when school let out. It was interesting to note the way the boys came down the street slamming about, shouting, and tripping each other up. It seemed to me there was one sort of youngster who had need to reform.

GETTING A LOAD OF SAWDUST BACK OF THE SAW-MILL

You find this variety in every village where half a dozen boys can get together. He talks in a loud voice when any witnesses or a stranger is about, is rude to his fellows, jostles them and orders them about, cracks crude jokes, either exceedingly pointless, or else of great age and worn threadbare, at which he himself has to do a good share of the laughing. He is, in short, showing off, and the show is a very poor one. He makes himself both disagreeable and ridiculous to most, and can only win admiration from a few weak-minded companions or overawed small boys. He is apt to grow into something of a bully among those weaker than himself, and to become, when older, a young man with a swagger.

It was October, the days were short, and I had early to seek a stopping-place for the night. It still lacked something of supper-time when I put my horse out at one of the farm-

A MEADOW STREAM

houses, and I took the opportunity for a walk on the village street. The damp gloom of evening had settled down. There were lights in the windows and movements at the barns, and a team or two was jogging homeward along the road. Westward, in plain sight across the river, was the heavy spur of a mountain, dark against the evening sky. A single little light was trembling on the summit of the crag. This came from a building known as "the prospect house." The proprietor lives there the year around, and from Sunderland's snug street, on cold winter nights, the light is still to be seen sending out shivering rays into the frosty darkness.

I returned presently to the house and had supper. That finished, the small boy of the family brought a cup of boiled chestnuts, and while we munched them, explained how he had picked up eighty-one quarts of nuts so far that year. In his pocket the boy had other treasures. He pulled forth a handful of horse-chestnuts, and told me they grew on a little tree down by the burying-ground.

"The boys up at our school make men of 'em," he said. "They take one chestnut and cut a face on it like you do on a pumpkin for a jack-o'-lantern. That's the head. Then they take a bigger one and cut two or three places in front for buttons, and make holes to stick in toothpicks for legs, and they stick in more for arms, and with a little short piece fasten the head on the body. Then they put 'em up on the stovepipe where the teacher can't get 'em, and they stay there all day. Some-

A DOOR-STEP GROUP

times they make caps for 'em." He got out his jack-knife and spent the rest of the evening manufacturing these queer little men for my benefit.

The next morning I turned eastward and went along the quiet, pleasant roads, now in the woods, now among pastures where the wayside had grown up to an everchanging hedge of bushes and trees. Much of the way was uphill, and I sometimes came out on open slopes which gave far-away glimpses over the valley I had left behind.

About noon I stopped to sketch one of the picturesque wateringtroughs of the region. There was a house close by, and a motherly looking old lady peeked out at me from the door to discover what I was up to. I asked if I might stay to dinner. She said I might if I would be content with their fare, and I drove around to the barn. An old gentleman and his hired man were pounding and prying at a big rock which protruded above the surface right before the wagon-shed. They had blasted it, and were now getting out the fragments. By the time I had my horse put out, dinner was ready, and we all went into the house. We had "a boiled dinner," — potatoes, fat pork, cabbage, beets, and squash all cooked together. The dish was new to me, but I found it quite eatable.

I was again on the road, jogging comfortably along, when I noticed two little people coming across a field close by. They walked hand in hand, and each carried a tin pail of apples. The boy was a stout little fellow, and the girl, a few sizes smaller, very fat and pudgy and much bundled up. I told them I'd like to take their pictures. They didn't know what to make of that; but I got to work, and they stood by the fence looking at me very seriously. I was nearly ready when a woman from the doorway of a house a little ways back called out, "Go right along, Georgie! Don't stop!" I told her I wanted to make their photographs — it wouldn't take but a minute. She said they ought to be dressed up more for that. But I said they looked very nice as they were, and hastened to get my picture. Then the two went toddling on. The boy told me there was a big pile of apples back there; also, as I was starting away, that his father had just bought a horse.

A ROADSIDE FRIEND

I took the sandy long hill way toward Shutesbury, a place famous for miles about for its huckleberry crops. It is jokingly said that this is its chief source of wealth, and the story goes that "One year the huckleberry crop failed up in Shutesbury, and the people had nothin' to live on and were all comin' on to the town, and the selectmen were so scared at the responsibility, they all run away."

The scattered houses began to dot the way as I proceeded, and after a time I saw the landmarks of the town centre — the two churches, perched on the highest, barest hilltop eastward. The sun was getting low, and chilly evening was settling down. Children were coming home from school; men, who had been away, were returning to do up their work about the house and barn before supper, and a boy was driving his cows down the street. I hurried on over the hill and trotted briskly down into the valley beyond, but it was not long before the road again turned upward. The woods were all about. In the pine groves, which grew in patches along the way, the ground was carpeted with needles, and the wheels and horse's hoofs became almost noiseless. There were openings now and then through the trunks and leafage, and I could look far away to the north-east, and see across a wide valley the tree-covered ridges patched with evergreens, and the ruddy oak foliage rolling away into ranges of distant blue, and, beyond all, Mount Monadnock's heavy pyramid. The sun was behind the hill I was climbing, and threw a massive purple shadow over the valley. Beyond, the ridges

BETTER THAN HOEING ON A HOT DAY

were flooded with clear autumn sunlight. Far off could be seen houses, and a church now and then — bits of white, toy-like, in the distance. The eastward shadows lengthened, the light in the woods grew cooler and grayer, and just as I was fearing darkness would close down on me in the woods, I turned a corner and the hill was at an end. There were houses close ahead, and off to the left two church steeples.

This was New Salem. The place had no tavern, but I was directed to one of the farm-houses which was in the habit of keeping "transients." There was only a boy at home. His folks were away, and he had built a fire in the kitchen and was fussing around, keeping an eye on the window in expectation of the coming of the home team. It arrived soon after, and in came his mother and sister, who had been to one of the valley towns trading and visiting. The father was over at "the other farm," but he came in a little later. Mrs. Cogswell told of the day's happenings, and

how she had found a knife by the roadside. It was "kind of stuck up," and she said she would bet some old tobacco-chewer owned it. However, Mr. Cogswell, having smelt of it, guessed not.

His wife now brought in a blanket she had bought at the "Boston Store," and we all examined it, felt of it, and guessed what it was worth.

Then she told what she paid, and how cheap she could get various other things, and what apples would bring.

As we sat chatting after supper, Mr. Cogswell took out his watch and began to wind it. It was of the Waterbury variety, and winding took a long time, and gave him a chance to discourse of watches in general, and of this kind in particular. Frank had such a watch, he said, and he took it to pieces and it was about all spring.

"You never saw such a thing," said Mrs. Cogswell. "Why, it sprung out as long as this table."

"Ho, as long as this table!" said Mr. Cogswell; "it would reach 'way across the room." He said his own watch kept very good time as a general thing, only it needed winding twice a day.

I was out early the next morning. The east still held some soft rose

THE BIG BARN-DOOR

tints, streaks of fog lingered in the valley, and the frost still whitened the grass. After breakfast I went northward, down through the woods and pastures, into Miller's valley. I followed a winding ravine in which a mountain brook went roaring over its uneven bed toward the lowland. I came into the open again at the little village of Wendell Depot. It was a barren little clearing, I found, wooded hills all about, a railroad running through, several bridges, and a dam with its rush and roar of water; a broad pond lay above, and below, the water foamed and struggled and slid away beneath the arches of a mossy stone bridge, and hurried on to pursue its winding way to the Connecticut. There was a wooden mill by the stream-side. It was a big, square structure with dirty walls and staring rows of windows. No trees were about, only the ruins of a burned paper-mill, whose sentinel chimney still stood, a blackened monument of the fire. There were a few of the plain houses built by the mill for its help, a hotel, some sand-banks, a foreign population, a dark, hurrying river, the roar of a dam, long lines of freight-cars moving through, and grim hills reaching away toward the sky.

From here I went westward, and in the early afternoon crossed the Connecticut River and began to follow up the valley of the Deerfield. I had to go over a big mountain ridge, but after that had comparatively level travelling. I went on till long after sunset, and presently inquired of a man I met walking if there were houses on ahead. He said Solomon Hobbs owned the nearest place, and lived up a big hill a ways off the main road. A little after I met a team, and concluded to make more definite inquiry. "Can you tell me where Mr. Hobbs lives?" I asked.

"Who, John?" he questioned as he pulled in his horse.

"No, Solomon," I replied.

"Oh, er, Solly! He lives right up the hill here. Turn off the next road and go to the first house."

It was quite dark now, and when I came to the steep, rough rise of the hill I got out and walked and led the horse. In time I saw a light

THE BOY AND RUNS AWAY

on ahead, and I drove into the steep yard. I had my doubts about stopping there when I saw how small the house and barn were. A man responded to my knock on the door and acknowledged to the name of Solomon Hobbs. He was a tall, broad-shouldered, long-bearded farmer, apparently about fifty years of age. He had on heavy boots and was in his checked shirtsleeves. He didn't know about keeping me overnight, but their supper was just ready, and I might stay to that if I wanted to. He directed me to hitch my horse to a post of the piazza and come in. On a low table was spread a scanty meal. Codfish was the most prominent dish on the board. After eating, I was ushered into the little parlor, for they had certain pictures of the scenery thereabout they wished me to see. Mr. Hobbs brought along his lantern and set it on the mantel-piece. It remained there though Mrs. Hobbs came in and lit a gaudy hanging-lamp. She was a straight little woman with short hair, rather curly and brushed up, wore earrings, did not speak

DIMPLES SUNLIGHT IN A "GORGE ROAD"

readily, and acted as if her head did not work first-rate. The little boy, who was the third member of the family, came in also. There was an iron, open fireplace with charred sticks, ashes, and rubbish in it. The carpet on the floor seemed not to be tacked down, and it gathered itself up in bunches and folds. The sofa and marble-topped centre-table and many of the chairs were filled with papers, books, boxes, and odds and ends.

There was some doubt as to where the pictures were, and it required considerable hunting in books and albums and cupboards and boxes and top-shelves to produce them. I did not notice that they put up any of the things they pulled down. Mr. Hobbs said of his wife that she had been in poor

health for a year past, and hadn't been able to keep things in order. When I had examined the pictures I got ready to start on. Mr. Hobbs said there was a hotel a mile up the road. I unhitched my horse, and the little boy, with a lantern, ran before me and guided me through the gateway.

At the hotel, when I had made the horse comfortable in the barn I betook myself to the bar-room, where a brisk open fire was burning. A number of men were loafing there, most of them smoking. One was a tall, stout-figured man who was always ready to back his opinion with a bet of a certain number of dollars, and quoted knowledge gained a year when he was selectman to prove statements about the worth of farms.

The proprietor of the place was a young man, with small eyes rather red with smoke or something else, a prominent beaklike nose, a mustache, and receding chin. He had an old, straight, short coat on, and he had thin legs, and looked very much like some sort of a large bird. He had a very sure way of speaking, and emphasized this sureness by the manner in which he would withdraw his cigar, half close his little eyes, and puff forth a thin stream of tobacco smoke.

In the morning I was out just as the sun looked over some cloud layers at the eastern horizon and brightened up the misty landscape. I left the hotel, and soon was on my way up the Deerfield River into the mountains. It was a fine day, clear at first, and with many gray clouds sailing later. I jogged on up and down the little hills on the road which kept

THE VILLAGE GROCERYMAN

along the winding course of the river. All the way was hemmed in by great wooded ridges which kept falling behind, their places to be filled by new ones at every turn. The stream made its noisy way over its rough bed, and every now and then a freight train would go panting up the grade toward the Hoosac Tunnel, or a passenger train in swifter flight would sweep around the curve and hurry away to the world beyond.

A little off the road in one place was a log house, a sight so unusual in old Massachusetts that such rare ones as one may come across always have a special air of romance and interest about them. This had a pleasant situation on a level, scooped out by nature from the lofty ridge which overshadowed it. It was made of straight, small logs, laid up cob-fashion, chinked with pieces of boards and made snugger with plaster on the inside. It had a steep roof of overlapping boards, through which a length of rusty stovepipe reached upwards and smoked furiously. There was a spring before the door, which sent quite a little stream of water through a V-shaped trough into an old flour-barrel. There were some straggling apple-trees about, and behind the house a little slab barn. Inside was a bare room, floored with unplaned boards. There was a bed in one corner, a pine table in another, and a rude ladder led to a hole in the upper flooring, where was a second room. The only occupant then about was cooking dinner on the rusty stove. Light found its way through two square windows and through certain cracks and crevices in the wall.

I followed the rapid river, on, up among the wild tumble of mountains which raised their gloomy rock-ribbed forms on every side. The regions seemed made by Titans, and for the home of rude giants, not of men. Presently a meadow opened before me, and across it lay the little village of Hoosac. The great hills swept up skyward from the level, and here and there in the cleared places you could see bits of houses perched on the

dizzy slope, and seeming as if they might get loose and come sliding down into the valley almost any day.

At the tunnel was a high railroad bridge spanning the river, a long freight train waiting, a round signal station, a few houses, and the lines of iron rails running into the gloomy aperture in the side of the hill. This was in a sort of ravine, and so somewhat secluded and holding little suggestion of its enormous length of over four miles. Some sheep were feeding on a grassy hillside just across the track, and looking back upon them they made a very pretty contrast to the wild scenery. The hills mounded up all about; the sun in the west silvered the water of the rapid river; a train waiting below the iron span of the bridge sent up its wavering white plume of smoke; and here on the near grassy slope were the sheep quietly feeding.

The road wound on through the same romantic wildness; now a mountain would shoot up a peak steeper and higher than those surrounding;

but none of them seemed to have names. As one of the inhabitants expressed it, "They are too common round here to make any fuss over."

In the late afternoon, after a hard climb up the long hills, I passed Monroe Bridge, where in the deep ravine was a large paper-mill. The road beyond was muddy and badly cut up by teams, and progress was slow. I expected to spend the night at Monroe Church, which I understood was three miles farther up, but I got off the direct route and on to one of the side roads. The sun had disappeared behind the hills and a gray gloom was settling down. The road kept getting worse. It was full of ruts and bog-holes. Like most of the roads of the region, the way followed up a hollow, and had a brook by its side choked up with great boulders. I came

THE OLD WELL-SWEEP

upon bits of snow, and thought there were places where I could scrape up a very respectable snowball.

After a time I met a team and stopped to inquire the way to the church, and the distance. The fellow hailed had a grocery wagon, and no doubt had been delivering goods. He seemed greatly pleased by my question; in fact, was not a little overcome, showed a white row of teeth beneath his mustache, and he quite doubled up in his amusement. He said he did not know where the church was; and he guessed I wasn't much acquainted up in these parts; said he wasn't either. He stopped to laugh between every sentence. He apparently thought he was the only man from the outside world who ever visited these regions, and now was tickled to death to find another fellow had blundered into his district. There was no church about there, he said; I must be pretty badly mixed up; this was South Readsboro', Vermont. "This is the end of the earth," he said. He kept on laughing as he contemplated me, and I got away up the road as soon as I could, while he, still chuckling to himself, drove down.

The snow patches become larger and more numerous, and soon I came into an open and saw a village up the hill. This was October, and the sight ahead was strange and weird. The roofs of the buildings were white with snow; there were scattered patches of it all about, and a high pasture southward was completely covered. It seemed as if I had left realities behind; as if in some way I was an explorer in the regions of the far north; as if here was a little town taken complete possession of by the frost; as if no life could remain, and I would find the houses deserted or the inhabitants all frozen and dead. There was a little saw-mill here and some big piles of boards; everywhere marks of former life; but the premature frost seemed to have settled down like a shroud on all about. I entered the village and found a man working beside a house, and learned from him that I had still three miles to travel before I came to the church.

I took a steep southward road and led the horse, with frequent rests, up the hills. Darkness had been fast gathering, the unset colors had faded, one bright star glowed in the west, and at its right a gloomy cloud mass reached up from the horizon. The neighboring fields got more and

HAYING TIME

more snow-covered, until the black ribbon of the muddy road was about the only thing which marred their whiteness. There were rocky pastures about, intermitting with patches of woodland. Here and there were stiff dark lines of spruce along the hilltops, and these, with the white pastures, made the country seem like a bit of Norway. Snow clung to the evergreen arms of the spruces and whitened the upper fence-rails, and the muddy trail of the road ceased in the crisp whiteness.

I was going through a piece of woods when I saw a house ahead with a glow of light in a window. I went past the friendly light. The dreary road still stretched on. No church was in sight, and I drew up and ran back to the house. A man came to the back door with a lamp. He said it was still two miles to the church, and I asked if I might stay overnight. Soon I had my horse in the yard and was comfortably settled by the kitchen fire. The kitchen was large, but the long table, the stove, a bed, and the other furniture made it rather cramped when the whole family were indoors. There were grandpa, and grandma, and "Hen" and his wife, and "Bucky," and "Sherm," and "Sis," and Dan, and little Harry, not to mention a big dog and several cats. After supper, grandma fell to knitting with some yarn of her own spinning; grandpa smoked his pipe and told bear stories; "Hen" mended a broken ramrod so that his gun might be ready for a coon hunt he was planning; Mrs. "Hen" sewed; "Sherm" and "Bucky" were in a corner trying to swap hats, neckties, etc., and "Sis" was helping them; Dan ran some bullets which he made out of old lead-pipe melted in the kitchen fire; and Harry circulated all about, and put the cats through a hole cut for them in the cellar door, and climbed on the chairs along the walls, and picked away the plastering at sundry places where the lath was beginning to show through.

Bedtime came at nine and I was given a little room partitioned off in the unfinished second story. In the first gray of the next morning a loud squawking commenced outside of so harsh and sudden a nature as to be quite alarming to the unaccustomed ear. Later I learned this was the flock of ducks

THE STREAM AND THE ELMS IN THE MEADOW

and geese which had gathered about the house to give a morning salute. The wind was whistling about, and came in rather freely at the missing panes in my window. As soon as I heard movements below I hastened downstairs. The two fellows in the bed in the unfinished part adjoining my room were still snoozing, and there were scattered heaps of clothing about the floor.

There was no one in the kitchen, and though the stove lid was off, no fire had yet been started. I heard old Mr. Yokes out in the back room.

UNDER THE OLD SYCAMORE

"'Bout time ye was gettin' up," he called to me.

"Yes," I said, "I heard you stirring, and thought it must be about time to turn out."

"Oh, it's you, is it? I thought 'twas one of the boys. They didn't bring in no kindlings last night."

He sat down by the stove and went to whittling some shavings. He had not yet got on either shoes or stockings. One by one the rest of the

AUGUST

family straggled in, and the fire began to glow and the heat to drive out the frostiness of the kitchen atmosphere. Outdoors the weather was threatening, and there were little drives of sleet borne down on the wings of the

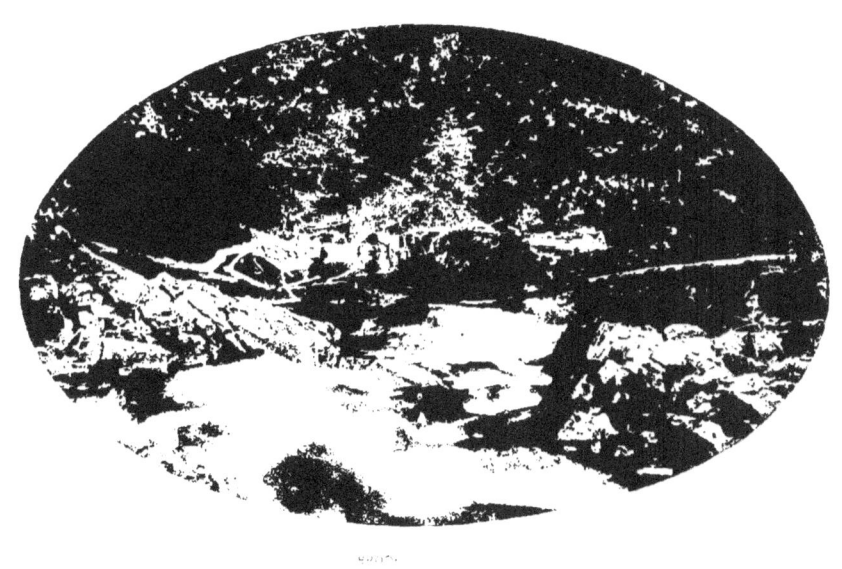

wind. After breakfast I concluded to leave this land of winter and followed down one of the steep roads into the autumn region of the Deerfield valley. By brisk travelling I succeeded by close of day in getting to the quiet meadows along the Connecticut. It had been a five days' journey. I saw only a little patch of New England, and the description is necessarily fragmentary; but at least there is presented characteristic phases of its nature and life as the traveller on a leisurely journey may see them.

PART IV

CAMPING AMONG THE NEW ENGLAND HILLS

IT was a warm night of midsummer. In a secluded hollow of the Green Mountain ranges of lower Vermont was pitched a small white tent. A half-moon was shining softly through the light cloud-hazes overhead, and had you been there, you could have made out the near surroundings without much difficulty. Tall woods were all about, but here was a little open where grasses and ferns and low bushes grew in abundance, and on a chance level of the steep, uneven hillside the campers had pitched their

tent. In the deep, tree-filled ravine close below was a stream, whence came the sound of its fretting among the rocks, and from a little farther up the solemn pounding of a waterfall. From the other direction came a different sound. It was the gentle clinking of a hammer on an anvil.

THE NEW ENGLAND COUNTRY 83

A RAINY SUMMER DAY

On the farther side of the narrow strip of woods, which shut it from sight, was a farmhouse, and it was thence came the sound of hammering.

The tent has two occupants. They are both young fellows, who had on the day previous started from their Boston homes for a vacation trip to the woods. In the city they were clerks, — one in a store, the other in a bank. The chance that brought them to this particular spot for their vacation was this: a school friend of theirs, who was blessed (or perhaps otherwise) with more wealth than they, and who was next year to be a senior in Harvard, had informed them a few weeks previous that his folks were going to the Groveland House for the summer. This, he said, was in the centre of one of the prettiest and most delightful regions of all New England, and he urged his friends, Clayton and Holmes, to by all means go along too. He expatiated on the beauties of the place with such an eloquence (whether natural or acquired at Harvard, I know not) that these two gave up the idea of a trip they had been planning down the coast and turned their thoughts inland.

But when they came to study the hotel circular that Alliston gave them, and noted the cost of board per week, this ardor received a dampener.

"Phew!" said Holmes, "we can't stand that. I don't own our bank yet."

"No, we can't, that's a fact," said Clayton. "I'd want more of a raise in my pay than I expect to get for years before I could afford that sum. The dickens! I thought these country places were cheap always —

AT WORK IN HER OWN STRAWBERRY PATCH

and here's a little place we've never heard of that charges more than half our big hotels here in Boston."

"Well, we've got to give up that idea, then," Holmes said. "I suppose, though, we might find a place at some farmhouse that wouldn't charge too high."

"The trouble is," Clayton responded, "that I don't like to go poking off into a region where we don't know a soul, and take our chances of finding a comfortable stopping-place at the right price. Then, you see, it's going to cost like anything getting there — just the fare on the railroad. I don't know as we ought to have considered the thing at all."

SEPTEMBER

"I hate to give it up," said Holmes. "We've seen a good deal of the shore, but have had hardly a sight of the country. It would be a great thing, for a change, to take that trip to Vermont. Now, why couldn't we try camping out? That's what the youngsters do in all the small boys' books I've ever read. We're rather older than the boys who were in the habit of doing that sort of thing in the books. But then, you know, that may be a good thing. It may have given us a chance to accumulate wisdom sufficient to avoid those hairbreadth adventures the youngsters were always having. They are good enough to read about, but deliver me from the experience."

"Harry," said Clayton, "I believe that's a good idea."

The conversation and thinkings necessary to settle the details were many and lengthy, and I forbear repeating them. The long and short of it is that on Monday, August 14, in the earliest gray of the morning, they were on the train that was to carry them to the Vermont paradise they had in mind.

EVENING

John Clayton, as luck would have it, worked in a dry-goods house, and therefore in planning a tent he was enabled to get the cloth for its makeup at a trifle above cost. He and Harry made numerous visits to the public library on spare evenings and consulted a variety of volumes devoted more or less directly to the science of camping out. The amount of information they got on the subject was rather bewildering, but they simplified it down to a few things absolutely necessary to think of beforehand, and concluded to trust to commonsense for solving further problems.

"Sufficient unto the day is the evil thereof," said Harry, who attended Sunday school-regularly.

The cloth used for the tent was cotton drilling. John's mother sewed the strips together under his direction, and their landlady allowed him to set it up in the little paved square of yard back of the block, and there he and Harry gave it a coat of paint to make it waterproof. The whole thing did not cost three dollars, and, as the boys said, "It'll last us

A LOAD OF WOOD ON THE WAY UP TO THE VILLAGE

a good many seasons." Aside from their tent they purchased a small hatchet, a ball of stout twine, a few nails, a lantern, and some tin pails, cups, and plates, and several knives, forks, and spoons.

It had been a question just where their camping-place should be. "We can't very well pitch our tent in the hotel yard," said Harry. "That high-priced proprietor wouldn't allow it, I'm sure; and, besides, we shouldn't want to."

Another perusal of the summering-place circular disclosed the fact that it gave a list of the attractions of the region about, with certain comments thereon. Among the rest was noted a waterfall seventy feet high. It was amid surroundings, so the circular said, exceedingly beautiful and romantic (whatever that may be). The boys thought that style of place would suit them to a T, and Harry, who carried the circular about in his pocket, got it out at the bank the next day after this decision was arrived at and underscored this waterfall with red ink.

In the late afternoon of August 14th the two were set down, "bag and baggage," at the forlorn little station which was the railroad terminus of their journey. To the left was a high sand bluff, half cut away, crowned with a group of tall pines. A little up the tracks was a deep, stony ravine where a little river sent up a low murmur from the depths. This was spanned by a high railroad trestle, and when the train rumbled away across it and disappeared around the curve of a wooded slope, the boys watched the curls of smoke fade into thin air and felt a bit homesick. Beyond was a small freight-house, but no other buildings were in sight. It was a little clearing in the midst of the woods. The only path leading away was the road, which made a turn about the near sand bluff, and then was lost to sight. At the rear of the depot was a smart stage-coach, into which a group of people were being helped by a slick footman. This coach was an attachment of the Groveland House. "Were the young gentlemen bound for the hotel?"

"No," said Clayton, "we're not going to the hotel. Isn't there any other coach?"

"Oh, yes, but that leaves here at two o'clock. It has a long route through the different villages, over the hills, delivering the mail and other truck. If they waited for the four-thirty train they'd hardly get around before midnight."

"We're much obliged," said Clayton, and the two went back to the front platform and sat down on their baggage.

"We won't go up to that hotel if we have to pitch our tent here on the sand back of the depot," said John.

They heard the coach rattle briskly away up the road, and the depot-master stamping around inside. He came out presently, and after locking the front door approached them. "Expectin' some one to meet ye?" he asked. He was a stout figured man, with a smooth, round, good-natured face that won the boys' confidence at once.

"No," John said, "we don't know any one about here. We came on a little camping trip. You see in Boston there are horse-cars running every which way that take you anywhere you want to go, and I s'pose we've got so used to them that we never thought of having any trouble in getting to the place we wanted to go to, though this is out in the country."

A WATERFALL IN THE WOODS

"Oh, ye came from Boston, did ye? I kinder thought ye was city fellers. Guess ye'll find horse-cars in these parts about as scarce as hen's teeth — just about. Whare was ye thinkin' of goin', anyhow?"

"We were going to Rainbow Falls."

"Rainbow Falls? Well, now, you've got me. I do'no' as I ever heared of 'em. Where be they?"

Harry whipped out his circular. "Why, here they are," he said. "See! right here under this heading, 'Nature's Attractions in the Drives about Groveland,'" and he pointed to the line underscored with red ink.

A PANORAMA OF HILLS AND VALLEYS

The station agent set down the two lanterns he had in his hand and drew a spectacle case from his vest pocket. "Sho," said he, when he got his glasses adjusted, "'Rainbow Falls,' so 'tis. 'Surroundings exceedingly beautiful and rheumatic' — er, no, it's *romantic* it says, I guess; the letters is blotted a little. Seventy feet high, it says. Well, now, I don't know what that is, unless it's the falls over at Jones' holler. The hotel folks have gone and put a new-fangled name onto it, I guess. There never's been any 'rainbow' about it that I've ever heared of."

"Is it a good place to camp out, should you think?" asked John.

"Well, yes; pretty good, if you like it," was the reply. "Now, if you fellers want to get up there to-night, there's some houses up the road

A PASTURE GROUP

here a few steps, and I presume ye can hire some one to get ye up there if ye want to."

"How far is it?" Harry asked.

"I should say it was five miles or something like that," said the man; and he walked off down the track.

"Now," said John, "we must wake up. I see no signs of houses, but we'll follow up the road."

The result was that a short walk brought them to a little group of habitations, and they accosted a farmer boy who was weeding in a garden and made known their wants. He would take them up, he said, if his folks would let him.

"How much would you charge?" asked Harry.

"Well, I do'no'," said the boy. "It's goin' to be considerable trouble, and it's a good five miles the shortest way, and hard travellin', too, some of the way. I should think 'twould be worth thirty-five cents, anyhow."

"We'll pay you fifty," said John, "if you'll hurry up with your team."

"I'll have to ask ma first," the boy replied.

He went to the house, and the two outside heard a low-toned conversation, and a woman looked out at them from behind some half-closed blinds. Then out came Jimmy with a rush and said he could go. He took pains to get his hoe from the garden, which he cleaned by rubbing off the dirt with his bare foot before hanging it up.

"Have ye got much luggage?" he asked. "'Cause if ye have we c'n take the rack wagon. The express wagon's better, though, if ye haven't got much. That old rack's pretty heavy."

The lighter vehicle, which proved to be a small market wagon, was plenty large enough, and into that was hitched the stout farm-horse, and the three boys clambered up to the seat.

"Git up!" cried Jimmy, cracking his whip, and away they rattled down to the depot.

"Now," said Jimmy, "they's two ways of gettin' where you want to go, and when you get there they's two places where you can go to. The road over Haley's Hill is the nearest, but it's so darn steep I'd about as soon drive up the side of a meeting-house steeple."

"Then you'd rather go the other road, I suppose."

"Well, I do'no'; that's considerable more roundabout."

"You can do as you please," said John. "We'll risk it, if you will."

"I guess I'll go over Haley's Hill, then. But I reckon you fellers'll get shook up some. 'Tain't much more'n a wood-road, and they's washouts on the downhill parts and bog-holes where its level that they've dumped brush and stuff into. You'll have to walk up the steep parts. Don't you want something to eat?" he then asked. "I brought along a pocketful of gingerbread, 'cause I knew I shouldn't get home till after dark. Here," and he pulled out a handful of broken fragments, "better have some."

"Thank you," said John; "but we had a rather late lunch on the cars, and I don't think we'll eat again till we get the tent pitched. What was it you said about there being two places up there we could go to?"

The boy took a mouthful of gingerbread, and when he got the process of mastication well under way he responded, "Well, there's Jules', and there's Whitcomb's. Jules' is on one side of the brook and Whitcomb's is on the other. Jules is the Frenchman, ye know."

"Which place is best?"

OCTOBER

"I do'no' 'bout that. Whitcomb's is the nearest."

"We'll try the nearest place, I think."

"I guess we'd better tumble out now," said the boy. "We're gettin' on to Haley's Hill, and old Bill's gettin' kinder tuckered. Hold on! don't jump out now. I'll stop on the next thank-you-marm."

He pulled in his steed just as the wheels went over a slight ridge that ran across the road, and the three alighted. They were in the dusk of a tall wood of beech and birches that was almost gloomy, so thick were the trees and so shut out the light. The road increased in roughness and in steepness, and finally the boy at the horse's head called out, "I say, I guess you fellers better push behind there. Bill can't hardly move the thing, and he kinder acts as if he was goin' to lay down."

The campers made haste to give their support, and the caravan went jolting and panting up the slope till the leader let fall the bridle-rein and announced: "There, we're over the worst of it. Now, if I can find a good soft stone to set on we'll rest a minute, and then we'll fire ahead again, and I'll get ye to Whitcomb's in less'n no time."

A PASTURE GATE

Jimmy found a bowlder to his mind and began to draw on his stores of gingerbread again. The horse nibbled the bushes at the roadside. The campers took each a wagon wheel and leaned on that and waited.

"I guess we might get in now," said the boy, rising and brushing the crumbs off his overalls. "It's pretty rough ahead, but they ain't much that's steep."

There were stones and bog-holes to jolt over, but after a little they came on to a more travelled way, and presently Jimmy drew in his horse and said, "This is Whitcomb's house right here. That's his dog at the gate barkin' at us."

John went to the front door and rapped. He got no response, and concluded from the grasses and weeds that grew about and before it that front-door visiting was a rare thing at that house. A narrow, flagged walk ran past the corner to the rear. He followed it, and in an open doorway of the L, found Mr. Whitcomb reading a paper.

A ROAD BY THE STREAM

"A friend and myself would like to camp over in your pasture for a few days, if you don't object," said John.

"All right, go ahead," said the farmer. "If you behave yourselves, and put up the bars after ye so't the cows won't git out I ain't no objections."

"Thank you," said John. "We'll try to do that. Have you milk to sell? We'd like to buy a couple of quarts or so a day."

The man turned his head toward the kitchen. "Ann," he said, "how is that — can ye spare any?"

A tall, thin-faced woman came to the door. She carried a baby in her arms. "I don't think we have any milk to spare," she replied. "We raise calves, because I ain't well enough to tend to the milk and make butter, and they drink about all we have. And I have two children, and the oldest ain't much more'n a baby, and they have to have some. We'd like to accommodate you, but I don't see how we can."

"It's all right," John replied; "we will find some other place for our milk supply."

He returned to the team and they drove through a wide, rocky mowing lot till they came to a stone wall which was without a break, and entirely blocked the way. A pasture lay beyond.

"The falls," said Jimmy, "are right over in them woods t'other side of this pasture. If 'twasn't for this pesky stone wall I'd drive right over there with ye. We'd 'a' done better to 'a' gone to Jules'. His place is only a little ways straight over here, but it's a mile and more by the road."

"Well, we've travelled far enough for one day," said Harry. "Let's get our tent over into the pasture and pitch it there."

"Agreed," said John. "The sky has been cloudy all the afternoon, and it looks more like rain than ever now. I shan't feel easy till we get a roof over our heads."

They tumbled their bundles over the fence and made their driver happy with a half-dollar, with which he drove whistling away. He, however,

AT THE PASTURE GATE

informed them that "he guessed likely he'd get up to see 'em in a few days, if they didn't get sick of camping before that and clear out."

The campers dragged their bundles over to a low beech-tree a few rods distant, and beneath its spreading branches proceeded to erect their tent. Poles and pegs they cut in a thicket near by. Their chief trouble was the lack of a spade to make holes for the end poles in the hard earth. But they made the hatchet do the work, though the fine edge they had taken pains to put on it before leaving Boston disappeared in the process.

After the tent was up they got their things into it and spread their bedding. The next thing was to hunt up a spring to serve as a water-supply.

"You get out a lunch," said John, "and I'll fill this tin pail with water."

THE SHEEP PASTURE.

That was easier said than done. He stumbled about in the dusk over the rough pasture-land with its tangle of ferns and hardhack bushes, and the best he could do was to get a couple of pints of fairly clean water from a rocky mud-hole. Afterward he scooped the hollow deeper with his hands, hoping it would soon fill with clear water.

At the tent Harry had the lunch spread and had lit their lantern.

"Do you know what time it is?" he asked. "It's half-past eight. If we'd had any farther to go we'd have been in a fix. Is that all the water you could get? I'm dry as a desert."

"I'll get more after supper," said John. "I've tumbled half over the pasture and I can't find anything but bog-holes."

After eating, both went out, Harry with the lantern, John with two pails. The clouds overhead had thinned and the stars twinkled through in places. The lantern with its two attendant figures went zigzagging over the lonely pasture waste to the water-hole. It had not yet cleared, but they skimmed off enough with a pail-cover to slake their thirst. They did not say much as they wended their way back to the tent, but both had the feeling that camping out was proving a rather severe experience of pioneering.

"I'm dead tired," said Harry, as he flung himself down on the bedding inside. Let's turn in for the night."

A few minutes later Farmer Whitcomb, glancing across the field, saw the soft glow of the lantern through the canvas walls of the tent disappear, and remarked, "Well, they get to bed early for city folks, but I've always thought myself nine o'clock was about the right time." He cleared his throat, looked up to the sky to get a hint of to-morrow's weather prospects, and went in and locked the door. Soon his light, too, was out.

The last sound the campers heard was the wind fluttering through the beech leaves in the tree above. It was a great change from the city noises and surroundings with which they were familiar.

On the following morning the campers were out at sun-up. Harry went over to their particular mud-hole and succeeded in scooping up a pailful of water, but he had not gone five steps before his foot slipped on a dewy hummock and the pail went flying. He returned to the original source of water-supply, but there was no chance of getting more just then, and the

result was he wended his way across the fields and filled his pail at the Whitcomb well-sweep.

"It's no use," he said on his return, "we've got to get nearer water. If matters go on as they've begun we'll waste half our vacation over this one thing."

"Well, we'll look around after breakfast," said John. "I've been trying to make a fire, but everything's so soaked with dew you can't make anything burn. I wonder if they always have such dews up here. It's just as if we'd had a heavy rain. We'll have to get in our firewood the night beforehand."

"It's a cold bite again this morning, is it?" said Harry. "I tell you, we've got to study up this matter. We must reform some way. Why, we're getting right down to barbarism. By the way, how d'you sleep last night?"

"First-rate," John replied; "don't remember a thing, only I feel a little sore in spots this morning."

"That's it," said Harry; "same way with me. Feel's if I'd had a good licking. Now, see here." He rolled down the bedclothes and exposed the ground. "See those humps? There's a stone sticking up. Here's another. There's a stub where some little tree has been cut off, and there several sticks and natural hummocks of the earth thrown in besides. Why, the worst savage, unless he was drunk, would be ashamed to use such a bed."

"Well," said John, "let us be thankful that we've come through the thrilling experiences that we have so far met with alive; to-day we'll hustle around and find a new camping-ground, and in the future we'll live in a style properly becoming to our dignity as members of Bostonian civilization, etc. But, come now, you've been regarding that bed of torture long enough. Trials past are only so many myths and shadows. At any rate, that's what Solomon or some other wise fellow has said. What you want

SUNLIGHT AND SHADOW

to do is to fortify yourself for trials to come. Supposing we go over and see this Jules after breakfast."

"I found out how to get there from our landlord when I went over for water," said Harry. "There's a side road that leads down to a little grist-mill just above here, and at the mill there's a foot-bridge across the stream."

"Good!" said John; and after breakfast our campers went down to the mill, which, with the placid pond above, was completely closed in by the green masses of the forest. It was a gray little building, with mossy shingles, and broken windows and doors. There were boards missing here and there from its sides, and it was so old and rude it seemed a wonder it did not slide down the precipice it half overhung. It had not been used for some time — that was plain. Below it was a steep, irregular fall of rocks over which thin streams of water were tumbling. Across the ravine, at the summit of the cliff, was a low dam; but it leaked badly, and the water did not reach its top by some inches. Midway in the stream, at the dam, was a rocky island where grew a few stunted pines. A foot-bridge crossed to it from a lower door of the mill. Thus it was necessary to climb to the top of the island cliff, where another bridge swung high up over the narrow ravine to the farther shore.

The boys poked about the mill and the pond for some time and then crossed the bridges. But they were no sooner across than John exclaimed, "How that thing did sway and crack! I'd walk ten miles before I'd cross that rotten plank again."

"So would I," said Harry. "It fairly made my hair stand on end. A fellow wouldn't be good for much after he'd tumbled down into a ravine as deep and rocky as that, I guess. The waterfall must be close by here. I can hear it. But let's hunt up Jules first. His last name is La Fay, so Whitcomb said."

A faintly marked path led away through the woods, and the two followed it. Some distance beyond it opened into a highway. They saw no signs of habitations, but they followed the road until they met an ox-cart.

"Can you tell us where Mr. La Fay lives?" asked John of the young man who was guiding the slow team.

"Yes," said he, "you take a narrer little road that turns off into

NOVEMBER

the woods down here a piece. You don't live round in these parts, do ye?"

"No," replied John.

"I don't belong around here either, and I'm mighty glad of it."

"Why, what's the matter?" John asked.

"It's so darn lonesome. That's what's the matter. Nothin' but woods, with now and then a farm kinder lost in it. Nothin' goin' on. Everything draggin' along slow as this old ox-team. I've hired out to Deacon Hawes

THE VILLAGE ON THE HILL

for the season, but I shan't stay more'n my time out. You're campin' up round here, ain't ye? Allen's boy brought ye up last night, so I heard. Mebbe I'll drop in and see ye this evenin'. We've got some sweet-corn just ripenin' down at the place that might taste good to ye."

The campers told him they would be glad to see him, and said that they expected to be near La Fay's, at the falls. They took the road he had indicated. It led through a dense young forest. The trees interwove their branches overhead so closely that the sunshine with difficulty penetrated the foliage to fleck the damp depths below with its patches of light. A short walk brought them out of the woods into a good-sized clearing sloping down into a wooded valley. Down the hill was a long, squarish house, one end entirely unfinished, and brown with age and decay. The rest had at some remote period been painted white. In front was a row of maples, beneath which a calf was tied. Opposite the house was a weatherworn barn, and behind it a small shed with a chimney at one end. The big barn-doors were open, and Mr. La Fay was just rolling out his hay-wagon. He was apparently about thirty-five years of age — a handsome, powerfully built man, square headed and strong jawed. He wore a mustache, had dark, curly hair, and a pair of clear, gray eyes, which looked straight at one and that held sparks which could easily flash into fire. The boys stated their errand, and La Fay told them to choose any place they pleased for their tent and go ahead. He could furnish them milk, and a horse occasionally if they wanted to drive.

"You are close by the falls if you go over there beyond that piece of woods," he said; "and from our hill here you can see half the world."

He took them out on the ridge beyond the barn. It was indeed a

A MILL IN THE VALLEY

beautiful piece of country — mowing-lots and orchards and pastures close about, a broken valley far below, where a little stream here and there glinted in the sunshine, and, bounding the horizon, many great, forest-clad

hills. Here and there were far-away glimpses of hilltop villages, of which La Fay gave them the names and the number of miles they were distant. The boys were delighted.

"Now, the way for you fellows to manage," said Mr. La Fay, "is either to take my horse and wagon for your traps, or, if you haven't got too many, to lug them across the stream down here. You'll find an old road and a ford that you can wade across a little below the falls, if you're not afraid of getting your feet wet."

"We'll try that way," said John.

A little yellow dog which had been smelling around now began barking over something he had found a few steps down the hill.

"What's he got now, I wonder," said La Fay, going toward him.

On the grass lay the remnants of a big turkey, about which the dog was sniffing excitedly.

"That's my gobbler," said La Fay. "A fox must have got hold of him last night. See, back there where all those feathers are scattered about is where the fox jumped onto him. That's where he'd squatted for the night. Well, I'll have that fox one of these days. That little dog can't be beat for tracking. He's the best dog to start up partridges or hunt rabbits or anything of that sort you ever see."

The boys asked if they might borrow a spade, and while at the barn getting it a little girl came running out to them from the house. She was perhaps eight or nine years old, a stout, vigorous little person, resembling her father closely in features.

"That's the young one," said La Fay. "Have you got the dishes washed, Birdie?"

"Yes," she replied, and then stood looking curiously at the strangers.

"She does a good share of my housework for me," La Fay went on. "I do the washing and the butter-making myself, and I get a woman to help once in a while in baking and mending. I can make as nice butter as any woman in this county. Look at my hands. They're hard, but they're smooth and clean. A farmer's hands needn't be rough and rusty if he'll only use soap and water enough, and be particular about it. I work as hard on my farm as any man about here, and I'm often up half the night blacksmithing, but I don't believe there's a man in the town can show such hands as those."

He looked toward the girl once more and continued, "The young one's mother ran away from her home two months ago. I never want to set eyes on her again. We didn't get along over-well together, sometimes. She had a temper, and I had a temper. I tell you, I smoke, and I drink, and I swear like the Old Nick; but I don't steal, and I don't lie, and I don't get drunk. Mary was like me, only there were times when she'd take too much drink. Then she'd flare up if I went to reasoning with her. The week before she left, she caught up a big meat knife she'd been using and flung it at me so savage that if I hadn't dodged quicker'n lightning 'twould have clipped my head, sure. It stuck in the wall and the point broke off. Well, I must get to haying now; but come round to the house any time. If Birdie or myself ain't there, you'll find the key to the back door behind the blind of the window that's right next to it. Go right in whenever you please. I know you fellows are honest. I know an honest

A LOG HOUSE

man when I see him. I'd trust you with my pocket-book or anything. I don't care what church you go to, or if you don't go at all. I can tell what a man's made of by his looks. There's some folks that I wouldn't want to be on the same side of the fence with. I tell you, money and policy count for a great deal in this world. I despise 'em."

He turned to the little girl and said, "Run in and get your hat Birdie, we must get in two or three loads before dinner, if we can."

The campers with their spade went through the strip of woods La Fay had indicated, and found a pretty bit of pasture beyond. The falls were in plain hearing in the ravine below, and they found a little level just suited for the tent, and not far away a fine spring of clear, cold water. Lastly, they noticed that one corner of the lot was a briery tangle of blackberry vines that hung heavy with ripe berries. This they thought an undoubted paradise — every delight at their tent door. First they ate their fill of berries,

A FARMYARD GROUP

and then went down into the hollow. The bed of the stream was strewn with great bowlders. Around towered the full-leaved trees. A little above was the fall, making its long tumble down a narrow cleft of the rocky wall.

The boys made a crossing by jumping from rock to rock in the bed of the stream. Below, they found the ford and the old road, and went up the path and across the pasture to their tent. It was something of a task getting their traps over to the new camping-place, but by noon the white canvas was again in place and they had dinner. By aid of the spade they gave the end poles of the tent a firm setting, and they dug a trench on the uphill side of the camp to protect them from overflow in case of rain.

ON A MOUNTAIN CRAG

I will not attempt to more than catalogue their doings for the next few days. That afternoon they took a long tramp to the village to lay in fresh food supplies. They returned at dusk, and found the young man whom they had met with the ox-team that morning, at the tent door with a bag of sweet-corn. He assisted them in making a fire, and they had a grand feast for supper. The next day, which was Wednesday, they took a long drive over the hills to points of interest that La Fay told them about. Thursday was reserved for a trouting expedition. Friday they drove over to the Groveland House to see their college friend, Alliston.

"Well, fellows," he said, "how do you like it?"

"Splendid!" said the campers; "we're having a grand, good time. How do you get along here?"

"It's rather dull times, I think myself," said Alliston. "We talk, and talk, and play tennis, and have a grand performance every day or two over a drive or a clambake. But half the time I think we're making believe we're having a good time rather than really having it. I have an idea, some way, that you fellows are getting the best of it."

ONE OF THE GREEN MOUNTAIN PEAKS

Nearly every evening the campers had callers, and in their tramps and rides they made many interesting acquaintances. After lights were out

AMONG THE BIG HILLS

they usually heard the sound of the hammer and the wheezing of the bellows up at La Fay's little shop beyond the woods.

Saturday morning came. The campers were still in bed, but they were awake. It had been a very hot night.

"Poke your head out, will you, Harry, and see what the weather's going to be," said John.

Harry loosed a tent flap and looked out. "The sun's shining," he said, "but the west is full of clouds and looks like a shower."

"Well, let's not hurry about getting up. If we take the noon train for Boston we shan't get home much before midnight, and we may as well take it easy now."

They continued napping. Half an hour later a gloom as of approaching night settled down over the landscape, and there was a threatening grumble of thunder in the skies. The waterfall in the hollow took on a strange wailing note, rising and falling with the wind, and the rustling of the leaves of the near woods seemed full of premonitions. The air began to cool and little puffs of wind began to blow, and the boys turned out and poked around getting breakfast. Then came some great scattering drops of rain, followed by a mighty crash of thunder and a dazzling flash of lightning that seemed to open the flood-gates of heaven, and the rain came down in sheets. The air took on a sharp chill, and the boys got on their overcoats. The wind increased in force and shook the tent menacingly with its mad gusts. The flashing of the lightning and the heavy roll of the thunder were almost continuous, and through it all sounded the hollow mourning of the waterfall.

"I tell you," said Harry, as he sat crouched on a roll of bedding, "I haven't much confidence in our mansion for such occasions as this."

He had hardly spoken when something gave way, and down came the tent, smothering him in wet canvas. It was some moments before the two could disentangle themselves. They made unsuccessful attempts to repair the wreck, but finally had to be content to prop up the ridge-pole so that it would shed the rain from their belongings, while they secured an umbrella and scud through the storm to the house, which they reached half drenched.

"The young one" was sitting by the kitchen window. Her eyes were dilated and she looked frightened. She had her hands folded idly in her lap. That was unusual, for she was ordinarily very busy.

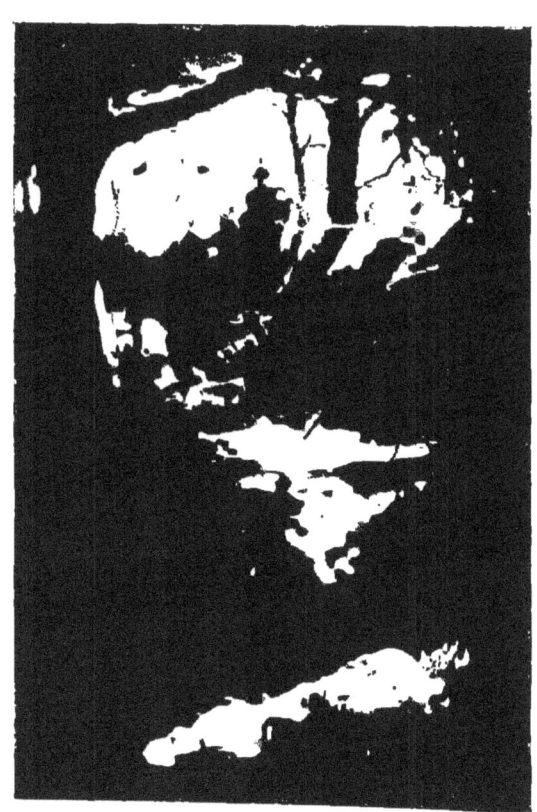

A DESERTED HUT IN THE WOODS

"You don't like these thunder-storms, do you?" said Harry.

Oh, she didn't mind them, she answered.

"Where's your father?" Harry asked.

"He went off down to the village before I got up. I guess he was going to get some flour."

"Then you've been all alone in this storm," Harry said.

She did not reply.

A fire was burning in the stove, and the campers hung their wet overcoats behind it, and themselves drew chairs to the stove and sat with their

feet on the hearth. On the table was a pile of unwashed dishes. From the large room next to the kitchen came the sound of dripping water. There was a great pool on the floor in one place, and two or three pans were set about to catch the streams trickling through the ceiling.

"This side of the roof always leaks when it rains hard," said Birdie. "Papa's going to fix it when he has time. I never seen it rain like it does to-day."

The shower was very heavy, but it did not last long. The clouds rolled away, and the sun shone down on the drenched earth from a perfect dome of clear, blue sky. Birds sang, and insects hummed and chirruped in the grasses, and the breezes shook little showers of twinkling water-drops from the trees. The air was full of cool freshness and sunshine. It seemed to give new life and cheer to every living creature. The campers were quite gleeful as they ran over to their tent after the storm was well past.

"We'll just hoist the ridge-pole into place," said John, "and let things dry off, and then we'll pack up."

The goods inside had escaped serious wetting, but they thought best to hang two of the blankets on some neighboring saplings.

"What a racket the water makes down in the gorge," said Harry. "Let's go down and have a look at it."

Everything was wet and slippery, and they took off shoes and stockings and left them at the tent.

"I declare!" exclaimed John, as they approached the stream, "this is a big flood. There's hardly one of those big bowlders but that the water covers clear to the top. How muddy it is! and see the rubbish! A

ROUGH UPLANDS.

man couldn't live a minute if he was to jump in there. How it does boil and tear along!"

"Come on, let's go up to the dam," shouted Harry, endeavoring to make himself heard above the roaring waters.

He clambered along over the rocks among the trees on the steep bank, but he had no sooner got within seeing distance than he stopped short and called excitedly to John close behind him, "It's gone! It's gone! The whole thing's washed away, — dam, and bridge, and mill, — all gone to smash. And see! the gorge at the fall's all choked up with big timbers. See the water spout and splash about 'em."

It was a grand sight — the mighty tumble of waters from the precipice above, foaming down into the gorge, then broken in the narrow, almost perpendicular, chasm into a thousand flying sprays, whence the mists arose as from a monster, steaming cauldron. And there the boys saw a rainbow which they had looked for in vain before. They stayed nearly an hour, fascinated by the turmoil of the flood.

"I suppose we've got to think about packing up," remarked John at last, with a sigh.

"It's a pity we can't stay around here another week," said Harry.

They climbed slowly up the wooded bank to the tent, pulled it to pieces, rolled all their belongings into snug bundles, put on shoes and stockings and went over to the house. As they approached they heard sounds of angry dispute. They turned the corner at the barn and stopped. La Fay was standing in the kitchen doorway. In the path before him stood a woman. She had on a pretty bonnet trimmed with gay ribbons. Over her arm hung a light shawl. Her face was thin, and there were blue lines beneath her burning black eyes. She stood sharply erect.

"Move on!" thundered La Fay, "and never show yourself here again."

"It's Mrs. La Fay," whispered Harry. "She's come back."

"Jules! Jules!" said the woman; and then her tones, either of excuse or pleading, dropped so low the boys did not catch the words.

"We'd better go back," suggested John.

"I say I want to hear no more," Jules continued fiercely. "The quicker you get off the premises, the better."

The woman looked at him in silence a moment, then turned short around and walked with quick steps away. La Fay stood frowning, with clenched fists, in the doorway. In the farther corner of the kitchen "the young one" was crouched in a chair, crying. The boys had turned away, but the drama had come to a sudden termination and they approached again.

DECEMBER

La Fay saw them. "She's been back," he said; "but I've sent her packing again. She came early this morning while I was away. She was here through the storm."

It was a painful subject, and John hastened to say that they had packed up ready to go to the train.

"My horse is out there by the barn hitched into my lumber-wagon,"

A PATH IN THE WINTER WOOD

said La Fay, "but I'll change him into the carryall. I'll be ready inside of ten minutes."

"All right, then." John responded; "we've got a little more to do to our bundles, and we'll be over there with them."

At the edge of the woods they looked up the road leading away from the clearing, and just beyond sight of the house they saw the woman again. Her arms were about her head, and she was leaning face forward against a big chestnut-tree. Once she clasped her hands and gave a sudden look upward. Then she resumed the former position.

The boys went down to their camp and did their final packing. The sunshine was becoming warmer. The wind was blowing more briskly, and it kept the grasses swaying and the leaves of the trees in a perpetual glitter of motion. In the aisles of the wood a thrush was chanting its beautiful song. From the hollow sounded the never-ceasing roar of the fall.

La Fay appeared, bundles were packed into the carriage, and they were off. They had just entered the road leading to the highway, when Harry spied a shawl lying at the foot of a tall chestnut. "What's that?" he asked.

La Fay drew in his horse and Harry jumped out and picked it up. He handed it to La Fay.

"Why," said the man, "that's Mary's. She must have dropped it."

WINDY WINTER—ON THE WAY HOME FROM SCHOOL

He laid it across his knee and said nothing for a long time. Indeed, they were more than half-way to the depot before he spoke more. Then he fell to stroking the shawl gently with his right hand and said, "Mary ain't done right. I know it; I know it. Poor girl! she's had a rough time since she's been away. I don't know but I ought to have been easier with her. And I like her still. I don't get over that, someway. I can't help it. If the past was blotted out, I'd do anything for her." He spoke all this slowly and meditatively.

Suddenly he straightened up. "Boys," he exclaimed, "I'll blot out the past so far as I can. I'll start new, if Mary will. I haven't been any too good myself. I know where she'll go to-day. I'll hunt her up on the way back."

With this resolution made he became quite jovial and talked very cheerfully all the distance to the depot. "Boys," said he, as he shook hands at parting, "I'm glad you've been up here. You're good fellows. I like to talk with you. Birdie, I know, will miss you a good deal, now you're gone. She told me only yesterday, 'I wish Mr. Clayton and Mr. Holmes would stay up here a long time, so I could learn to talk nice, the way they do.' If you ever get around this way again be sure to come and see Jules the Frenchman."

The train rumbled into the station at that moment, and the campers hastily bade a last adieu and were off.

www.ingramcontent.com/pod-product-compliance
Lightning Source LLC
Chambersburg PA
CBHW021938160426
43195CB00011B/1137